TURF
ACCOUNT

TURF ACCOUNT
Steve Smith Eccles
with Alan Lee

Macdonald
Queen Anne Press

A *Queen Anne Press* BOOK

First published in Great Britain in 1986 by
Queen Anne Press, a division of
Macdonald & Co (Publishers) Ltd
3rd Floor
Greater London House
Hampstead Road
London NW1 7QX

A BPCC plc Company

Jacket photographs — Front: George Selwyn
                                  Back: Gerry Cranham

British Library Cataloguing in Publication Data

Smith Eccles, Steve
    A jockey's diary.
    1. Steeplechasing — Great Britain
    I. Title   II. Lee, Alan, *1954–*
    798.4'00924   SF359.3.G7

    ISBN 0-356-12106-2

Typeset by Leaper & Gard Limited, Bristol

Printed and bound in Great Britain by
Hazell, Watson & Viney Limited
Aylesbury, Bucks

A Member of the BPCC Group

To Di, Sandra, George and Penny
who have to live with me!

Brushing through the birchwood switches
Cramming at the open ditches
Taking what the fate provides them
Danger calling death beside them
'Tis a game beyond gainsaying
Made by God for brave men playing.

WILL H. OGILVIE

INTRODUCTION

Time was, if you believe the old-stagers of the racing game, when every jump jockey was a little like Steve Smith Eccles. Frankly, I don't believe a word of it. There is something special about the pocket battleship from coal-mining country in Derbyshire: it is called flair. He shows it on and off the racetrack, and it sustains him through the varied scrapes and crises in which his extravagant lifestyle lands him.

Often infuriating, sometimes outrageous but never, ever boring, Steve is certainly a throwback to another age, and it is one of the great regrets of his life that, all too often, his own gregarious nature seems foreign to most of his contemporaries in the riding game.

'Ecc', as he is affectionately known within the weighing-rooms of England, shares some — but not all — of the traits of another great sporting extrovert, Ian Botham. He is a fighter, a survivor and an incurable adventurer, sometimes blind to the consequences but never short of motivation. Life, he believes, is for living hard and full, and if nobody else wants to join him, he will go ahead and do it all alone.

He drinks, sometimes too much. He drives, sometimes too fast. He is a nocturnal creature who can forget his cares and worries, his bumps and bruises, in the throes of a party. And because he has always managed to divorce the working side of life from play, because he has never allowed his social life to detract from his tough, competitive riding, he has reached the top of the tree and he can afford to spoil himself.

Suddenly, when John Francome retired in 1985, the punters

promoted Smith Eccles to favourite to be the next champion jockey. Steve took a deep breath and tried to ignore the implications. He had seen it all before, long ago, when he was a mere twenty-one-year-old and nowhere near as proficient. The reality had not matched the expectation then, and he did not intend to allow his feet to leave the ground this time.

For all his extravagances, he has become essentially a pragmatist. He grew up in an area where virtually everyone went down the pit. He was one of the fortunate few to stay above ground, and he has never allowed himself to forget his good fortune. There has always been an anxiety to prove himself in his chosen lifestyle, blended with an acceptance that, whatever tomorrow may bring, it can hardly be as grim as life might have become if he had trodden the traditional coal-mining path.

No one can say he has failed, despite the fact that, in the 1985-86 season, he still did not become champion. As in each of the preceding half-dozen years, he rode more than his share of big-race winners and finished in the top few. He was also involved in controversy, gossip and front-page headlines. Injured several times, his face was disfigured more than once. He had rows inside and outside racing, had desperate disappointments and days of high elation. All this he has faithfully chronicled in the following pages with a diligence and discipline that some would not suspect of him. Steve bared his thoughts in words, I put them on paper. We both hope the end result is worthy of the character at the centre of this story.

Alan Lee

JULY

SUNDAY 28 JULY

It's been an odd sort of summer. The new season is six days away and I feel as if I need a holiday more than anything. I'm knackered. Since the first day of June, eight short weeks ago, when last season's jumping programme ended, I have been on the go virtually non-stop. I have ridden in America, Australia, New Zealand, Belgium, Jersey and Ireland, and the occasional spells I have had at home seem to have consisted of a hectic round of parties. That's what comes of living in Newmarket, headquarters of flat racing, during their busy months.

Mind you, I'm not complaining. The close-season might have been exhausting, but it has undoubtedly been a success. I've ridden a few winners, gained a lot of experience, done myself some good in all kinds of ways. More than that, I've also had a good time, which is an important factor in my life. Perhaps I belong to a different age, an age when sportsmen counted the laughs first and the pounds later; certainly, I find myself increasingly alone among modern jockeys in the way I live my life. But I adhere to the simple, clichéd philosophy that you are only young once. I don't intend to allow my active years to slip past unused.

There is a lot to look forward to this season. On paper, indeed, my chances of success look better than they have ever done and I notice that the bookmakers are quoting me as low as 5-2 to be champion jockey. The odds, frankly, are ludicrous — it would be more realistic to give 5-2 against me getting through the season in one piece!

In National Hunt racing, you are constantly being reminded that you are only as safe as your last ride. Everyone has falls. They are an

11

unavoidable and inevitable hazard of the occupation. There is luck involved — the best jumpers can get brought down, or make one mistake and fall — and although good jockeys can to some extent see the pitfalls before they occur and so make their own luck, no one is immune from danger. All you can do, once you have attained the happy level of being able to pick and choose rides, is to pace yourself, turning down spare rides on notoriously bad jumpers just for the sake of another £46 fee. Better to refuse the cash and be fit for a winner tomorrow.

All too often, something will go wrong just when you kid yourself you are on top of the job. Racing is that kind of cruel leveller — it will build you up to a certain pitch and then knock you flat again with a single blow.

Success naturally spawns pressure. Even the expectation of success adds an extra strain. I will begin this season painfully aware that the racing public are expecting me to do well, indeed that many of them are expecting me to be champion. Hard as I will try to ignore it, that knowledge could affect my riding. It only needs a few things to go wrong, a little confidence to drain away . . . everyone is human.

The one certainty about the coming season is this. I don't know where it will happen and I don't know when, but more than once in the coming months I will experience genuine fear. There is no escaping it. Every jockey has his fear factor, every jockey will be frightened during a race several times in the course of a jumping season. The good ones can cope, conquer it and carry on as if it never happened. The bad cases never do. One jockey can always see fear in another. We know the tell-tale signs. Thankfully, it is seldom obvious to anyone outside the job, and nine out of ten jockeys will give up and get out as soon as they see the red light and realise their 'bottle' has gone. The few who try to battle on are a pathetic sight to see.

It is for these reasons, among others, that I cannot begin this diary with any brash predictions. I am not even thinking about winning the championship. With the retirement of my old mate John Francome, who was incomparable during his last few years of riding, the title race is likely to be more open than at any time since I started riding. A good start is important; weather will play its part; injuries could be decisive. Skill, of course, is a not insignificant factor, allied to the ammunition — in horse terms — to show it. Weighing all these things up, I reckon there are six perfectly good candidates for the crown: Jonjo O'Neill, Chris Grant and Neale Doughty in the north, Peter Scudamore, Hywel Davies and myself in the south. And I am perfectly prepared for someone outside this half-dozen to surprise us all.

One advantage of my working summer is that I will begin the season fully fit. There will be no holiday pounds to sweat off — I haven't had a holiday — and no race-rustiness to oil because I have hardly stopped race-riding.

It will not take me long to get back into the routine of the season, I'm sure of that. Although I feel tired now, a few meetings, hopefully a winner or two, and I will be back on auto-pilot. There are memories to keep me going, too. The summer has certainly filled in a few more pieces of life's rich tapestry and I have plenty of tales to tell in the weighing-room, arising from the world tour I undertook with the British jockeys team during June. Tales like the one about the young jockey who struck lucky with an Australian girl and was getting down to important matters in his hotel bed when a radio station announcer phoned, demanding an instant live interview about his winner at the big meeting that day. He managed to prove it is possible to do two things at once . . . !

So many things happened to me on that trip it is hard to know which to relate first. I recall being thrown in a Baltimore swimming-pool fully-clothed on my 30th birthday, the day after we had beaten the Americans; I remember being boldly chatted up on a plane across the States — by a male steward; I remember the L.A. women, the foul New Zealand weather, the stunning Australian hospitality. I shall never forget riding out in the darkness before dawn near Melbourne and I will certainly always cherish the memory of riding two big winners on the Saturday afternoon TV card at Moonee Valley. Most of all, it strikes me, I got used to being away from home. There were, of course, times during the three-week tour when every one of us got fed up, and one memorable occasion at Auckland airport when I threatened to get on the next plane back to London, but I did get used to the lifestyle, the confinements and the freedoms of hotel life, and the cameraderie which is naturally created in a travelling party of seven.

We all felt that we were riding for Britain, for Queen and Country, rather than simply for ourselves, and it was striking just what a difference this made. We celebrated each other's winners as if they were our own; we strained every muscle to pick up points for third or fourth place which just might swing a match; winning, as a team on faraway foreign soil, meant a lot. Team riding did have its amusing moments, of course. During the hurdle race at Moonee Valley, I was rounding the home turn on the favourite. Peter Scudamore was on my outer, beaten but battling for a place, and he suddenly yelled: 'One up your inner, Steve'. I moved across to close the gap and heard an unmistakeably Welsh scream. I had just cost my own team-mate Hywel Davies any chance of winning. Fortunately, I went on to win, but Hywel did not allow 'Scu' to forget . . . .

Being lucky with my weight, I could always tuck into a hearty bacon, eggs and brown sauce breakfast while Hywel and Peter set off for the sauna each morning. And, being naturally gregarious, I enjoyed the social life of being abroad, and usually outstayed my team-mates on our evenings out. I enjoyed all the good points of foreign racing, especially in America and Australia, but in New Zealand we saw things which made us all appreciate British standards. In a place called Tauranga we had to ride a hurdle race over obstacles which were literally five-bar gates staked into the ground. For the chases they simply added brush on top to create a homespun fence. Frankly, it was dangerous, and no English race-course would have contemplated such death-traps. We all came through unscathed, however, and I have since ridden in Jersey, Belgium and Ireland — all in the space of one hectic long weekend in mid-July.

Now I am ready and eager for the business of the home season. Today, I spoke to all the trainers who are likely to engage me on a regular basis, and I have to admit things look good. John Jenkins, always sure to run plenty of horses on the firm ground at the beginning of the season, ought to give me a good start as I will be sharing the work on his string with Simon Sherwood, last season's champion amateur; Nicky Henderson will not run many early on, but he has some impressive animals for when the season is seriously underway and I will ride 30 of the best; Jeff King, who provided me with a dozen winners last term, has more horses of a higher quality this time; my Newmarket neighbour Gavin Pritchard-Gordon will have his usual few nice jumpers; there will be Duke of Milan and Dark Hansel, two lovely horses, to ride for Nick Gaselee, and Kathies Lad — who won at both Cheltenham and Aintree in the spring — for Alan Jarvis ... yes, things look good. But despite my confident front, I never count my chickens. This time next week the season will be a day old and everything could look different after one fall.

MONDAY 29 JULY

You can never accurately predict the bad fall but you can take precautions to avoid it. Bill Clay, a nice guy who trains in Uttoxeter, phoned up today to offer me a ride on Saturday. It is a novice chaser having his first attempt over fences — on the first day of the season. I hate turning down rides but I had to refuse. What an idiot I would look if, with all the good horses I can look forward to riding this season, I broke my leg on that. Bill is not too happy, but there are times as a freelance when you just have to risk upsetting people.

AUGUST

SATURDAY 3 AUGUST

The season began with a race against time and traffic. Stayed last night with John Francome at Lambourn after flying back from Ireland, where I had a ride on Thursday. Set off in plenty of time for the drive down to Newton Abbot, I thought, even allowing for the inevitable Saturday morning West Country holiday traffic. But the M5 was worse than I've ever known it — bumper to bumper all the way. I watched the clock ticking on, imagined my fancied ride in the first being snapped up by somebody else, and decided it was time for action. My Porsche can travel a bit, given a clear run, so I opted for the hard shoulder and, with a wary eye in the mirror for flashing blue lights, cruised along at 95 mph.

It was some sort of journey, that. But I got to the course in time, won the first event on Kyoto and the third on The Owls. I could hardly have asked for a better start.

SUNDAY 4 AUGUST

Jonjo has broken his collarbone. I read it in the papers this morning and felt so sorry for the poor guy. He had a wretched time with injuries last season but, with Francome out of the way, he was favourite with many bookmakers to be champion this time. It didn't take long for fate to catch up with him again — his second ride at the Market Rasen evening meeting, on a moderate horse in a very moderate selling hurdle, and there he was back in hospital — out for maybe three weeks. It could have been me; we tread a very fine line between success and disaster in this game.

MONDAY 5 AUGUST

Just one ride, which did not oblige. But I have had a good week-end staying, as usual, at the Palace Hotel in Torquay. It must be six years now since I began to camp here for the early-season Devon meetings and I always look forward to coming back. The facilities are vast and include tennis courts inside and outside, on which Francome and I have challenged all-comers every autumn. If it doesn't seem quite the same so far this year it must be because John is not here with me. We share a similar sense of humour and outlook on life; I miss him a lot. I also have a feeling that he is pining, too. When I stayed with him last week it was not the normal bouncy 'Franc'. It struck me then that he might be miserable because he would be missing out on Devon this year ... but then again, maybe he was just worried about his imminent new life in training. I caught him reading a book called 'How to train racehorses', which should amuse the boys!

The hospitality the Palace staff always show to me was illus-trated again tonight. I got back to the hotel, after having some dinner, around 11.30 p.m. and noticed that the water pump on my car was leaking. The hotel manager immediately summoned one of his garage staff and the fault was fixed on the spot while the manager bought me a drink in the bar — very civilised.

Mind you, life has had its literally painful moments at the Palace. About five years ago, I went to the traditional start-of-season ball always held down here after the opening day at Newton Abbot. A footloose bachelor, I took a fancy to two different girls at the ball; one had to be given the elbow and she did not take it well. The following day I had a message to say she was waiting for me in the lobby of the hotel and when I strolled down to see her it was obvious that time had not healed. She had brought along a friend and, with a face like thunder, she gave me little time for explanations. I could tell she was about to hit me. I threw up an arm to catch the intended blow and was just telling her to be sensible when I got stars before my eyes as what felt like a paving slab hit me on the back of my head. Concentrating on one potential assailant, I had unwisely ignored her mate, who had slipped round behind me and swung her handbag with regrettable accuracy. I can only assume that, with malice aforethought, she

17

had slipped something blunt and heavy inside it as it gave me a fierce headache, not to mention an entirely undeserved reputation with the giggling reception staff of the Palace .... .

TUESDAY 6 AUGUST

I agreed to drive to Finmere, a 390-mile, six-hour round-trip from Torquay, for a Jockeys' Show Jumping event today. Under normal circumstances I would not have gone but this year the proceeds are all going to the appeal fund set up for Bob Woley, an ex-jockey. I knew it was a good cause, and this morning 'Franc' and I went to see Bob in the spinal injuries unit of Stoke Mandeville Hospital, and the visit had quite an effect on me.

I remembered Bob as a big bull of a man, a character much liked and enjoyed by all his fellow jockeys. Now, after a fall which has paralysed him and taken away the great love of his life, he is a shadow of his old self. For a change, sitting there in his company, I was entirely lost for words, welcoming the chatter of 'Franc', who had seen Bob in that state before. It could happen to any of us riding today, and if I ever ended up in that position I don't think I would want to go on living. I drove on to Finmere in a mood of near depression; but I was glad I had decided to go.

WEDNESDAY 7 AUGUST

I always say that the most hazardous part of my job is not riding horses over obstacles but having to contend with some of the other lunatics who are somehow let loose on our jumping courses. The situation is often at its worst in the West Country, where a number of Devonshire farmers, not to mention their sons and daughters, ride the family horses and any others they are allowed to sit on. Some ride like cowboys, apparently imagining they are acting in a particularly violent western and that the other jockeys in their race are all Indians. There are a couple of girls in particular who ride down here and should undoubtedly be locked up as dangers to civilisation. Today on the Devon course on Haldon Hill the weather was consistent with our worst summer in years — hosing down with rain — and the recipe for accidents only needed the addition of the cowboys. Rain on firm ground creates a surface like an ice-rink and guiding a horse round bends in such conditions is tricky enough without the crazy, untutored riding of some of this lot. They took no notice at all of the conditions, however, and I was very grateful indeed to come through the day not only in one piece but also with a third winner chalked up.

Although all three winners have been for John Jenkins, I am having to bite my tongue over the situation, as neither Simon Sherwood nor I ever quite know which horses we are supposed to ride. It is frustrating, of course, but most jockeys would give a lot to have a share of the Jenkins stable's early action, so it is best to say nothing.

Simon also rode another winner today and he is emerging as one of the old school. Apart from being a very tidy rider, he is a nice fellow who is far from reluctant to have a night out on the town. I had begun to wonder if I was the last of the breed!

THURSDAY 8 AUGUST

Most jockeys will tell you they very seldom hear the noise of the crowd when they are riding a race, and I am usually no different. But there is an exception to every rule. I rode a horse called Sailing By, running for the second day in succession and attempting a hat-trick of wins in the first four racing days of the season. He failed spectacularly. At Devon's very first hurdle, the horse made such a bad mistake that his nose hit the ground and I slid forward out of the saddle until I was no more than a foot from the ground, clinging onto the horse's neck with my head under his. I was convinced I had gone past the point of no return and I could clearly hear the jeers of the crowd as the horse — heavily backed to favourite — galloped past the stands with his jockey in this desperate and undignified position. Using all the strength and balance I could muster, I somehow struggled slowly onto the horse's back and as I slipped into the plate, the jeers turned to cheers and a thunderous round of clapping broke out as many substantial wagers were, at least temporarily, rescued. All this had hardly helped Sailing By's prospects, though, and combined with it being his third race in a week, I was far from disappointed to finish fourth after such a hairy adventure.

When it is cold and raining, as it was today, Haldon is one of racing's most uninviting places and I was just warming myself in the bar with the day's first whisky after racing when I happened to overhear a conversation. It was plainly a mother talking to her daughter; equally plainly, they did not know who I was, as mother was in the middle of giving daughter her views on Simon Sherwood, which went something like this: 'He's a very nice boy, dear, but what a pity he spends so much time with that Steve Smith Eccles ... he'll ruin him, you know.' I briefly considered introducing myself, but I'm not one to cause unnecessary embarrassment!

FRIDAY 9 AUGUST

Checked out of the Palace this morning after a six-night stay. It cost me around £200 but I consider it money well spent. I feel fresh and relaxed and I have enjoyed the first week of the season without the strain imposed by constant driving. With four meetings in this part of the world, I would have thought it logical to stay down but I am obviously in the minority. I compare my approach with that of Richard Rowe, Josh Gifford's stable jockey. Richard lives in Findon, West Sussex, a four-and-a-half-hour drive from either of the Devon courses, and he has ridden at each of the four meetings this week, yet commuted every day. On petrol costs alone he can hardly have saved any money, and with four nine-hour round trips I very much doubt if he has actually enjoyed the opening week of a long season. On Saturday, he got so badly caught in the traffic that he missed his first two rides, but even then he didn't reconsider and stay down for the other meetings. I know it takes all sorts, but I really can't understand it.

SATURDAY 10 AUGUST

Last season it took me two months to ride my first four winners. This time I have reached that figure already after winning on Celtic Story in the novice chase at Worcester tonight.

We have evening meetings at each end of the jumping season and I think it is fair to say that they are more popular with the public than the jockeys. They attract big crowds because more people can come along after work (or, in the case of a Saturday, after a day in the garden, at the shops or under the wife's thumb) but as far as the jockey is concerned it means a late finish, probably no dinner, and perhaps a long drive home in the dark.

My own drive home this evening was eventful. I was moving at a decent speed through Alcester, the first town out of Worcester, when I saw a gorgeous blonde hitching a lift on the pavement. I screeched to a halt 20 yards or so further on and watched in the mirror as this attractive creature tripped along the road and hopped in next to me. Only then, at close quarters, did I realise I had made a grave mistake. The blonde turned out to be a fellow in drag. It gave me the shock of my life but I proceeded to give 'him' the shock of his, driving him on to Stratford at an alarming speed before gratefully depositing him and continuing on my way with a silent vow to be more careful of future hitch-hikers.

SUNDAY 11 AUGUST

There is no real day of rest once the season gets properly underway. During August and September, when the meetings are scattered, we all have a few days off now and again, but once the time comes, during October, for racing every day, it is a seven-day-a-week existence, Sundays being the day on which most jockeys plan their week ahead. Even today, I spent two-and-a-half hours on the phone to my trainers, only to discover that none of them — with the exception of John Jenkins — has anything close to being ready to run. John, of course, has had another tremendous start with nine winners in eight days, and no other trainer even tries to compete with his striking rate at this end of the season.

Sunday lunch is a luxury, a time when I greatly appreciate having very few weight problems, and after indulging myself with the joint and the roast potatoes I set to work in the garden — and not at all unwillingly. Gardening may be a chore to many, but to me it is a release. I love trees and plants and take great pride in tending my acre, even though I do pay a regular gardener, a World War II bomber pilot named Joe Pryor, to look after it. For me, it is a rare chance to switch off from racing.

WEDNESDAY 14 AUGUST

The glamour of this life is not even skin-deep. Having set off early this morning, heading for Fontwell, I was caught in the rush-hour chaos around the Dartford Tunnel. We were stationary for half-an-hour and time was beginning to run short, so for the second time this season I took to the hard shoulder. This time I was not so lucky — a police car appeared, followed by the notebook, and all my protestations about being a jockey late for work had no effect at all. I didn't have the nerve to adopt the tactics of one controversial colleague of mine who, when stopped on the motor-way for driving at 105 mph and told he would probably lose his licence for it, glibly replied that it made no difference at all to him as he was a leukaemia sufferer with only a few months to live. The poor, duped policeman took pity and put his notebook away.

After all the fuss, I raced into the Fontwell weighing-room half-an-hour before my race wondering if the hassles of my life-style were all worthwhile. Then I went out and won on The Somac and, instantly, I knew they were.

THURSDAY 15 AUGUST

Rode two losers, back at Newton Abbot, including Celtic Story, which fell five out in the novice chase. He wouldn't have won anyway, but I spent some time thinking back through the incident and apportioning blame. It is important always to assess why you have had a fall, particularly if you are likely to be riding the horse again. I am very self-critical about my riding but I believe it is the only way to improve. No one ever stops learning in this game and if you have made a mistake, such as giving a horse a kick into the fence when you should have been taking a pull, then try to correct it the next time.

FRIDAY 16 AUGUST

John Jenkins and Philip Mitchell both train at Epsom and it would be fair to say that they don't see eye to eye. They are about the same age, both have tasted success and both are strong-willed ... all of which helps to explain the remarkable scenes in the foyer of the Plumpton weighing-room today, when I am convinced they would have come to blows if I had not stepped in. The argument arose because both had a runner in the three-year-old hurdle and both believed they had booked Simon Sherwood to ride. Simon, having been advised yesterday morning that John would not be running his horse Asticot, had agreed to ride Billion Boy for Philip. Some time between 9.30 and 10.00 a.m. yesterday, however, John obviously changed his mind and Asticot appeared among the declarations, S. Sherwood's name next door. Poor Simon, who was just the pawn in this affair, found himself with two rides and neither trainer was prepared to release him.

Philip was the first of the pair to arrive at Plumpton and duly made out his declaration sheet for Billion Boy with Simon down to ride. When John arrived, he ripped up Philip's sheet and wrote out his own, naming Simon. I observed all this, and with interest, because I thought one of them would ask me to deputise on their horse, so it came as something of a blow when they seemed willing to ignore S. Smith Eccles and fight over S. Sherwood.

John lost his temper first, only yards away from the stewards' room and close to disaster. I moved in to an argument which had nothing at all to do with me and told him to calm down, because if he started a fight he would lose his licence (and, although I refrained from saying so, this meant I would lose rides!). Fortunately, he saw sense, backed down and told me to ride Asticot, which unfortunately got beaten ... by Billion Boy. Philip diplomatically said later that he and John were friends again, but I am not so sure.

Another eventful day at least provided a winner, Kyoto hacking round to win the handicap chase under 12 stone 8 pounds. He is the best two to two-and-a-half-mile chaser around at this time of year, and we are trying to get him invited to America for the Colonial Cup — another trip to look forward to.

SATURDAY 17 AUGUST

With no rides at the two meetings, Bangor and Market Rasen, I took the chance of a rare Saturday off — well, nearly off. I was still up and out of the house by 7.00 a.m. to school some horses for Gavin Pritchard-Gordon, but the rest of the day was my own.

SUNDAY 18 AUGUST

I made the most of my free day and enjoyed myself rather too much, judging by my head this morning. Last night's dinner party was lively and lengthy and I am paying the price. I often spend some time on Sundays reflecting on the week gone by, and I have little to complain about today, the hangover apart. I've ridden two more winners this week and survived my first fall of the season, always an important landmark to pass. Simon and I have each ridden six winners now, which is the sort of start to boost confidence. I find it very noticeable in the weighing-room that there are still plenty of tense faces; a lot of jockeys fancy their chances of being champion this season, and they are all champing at the bit, trying to get those first few winners under the belt.

MONDAY 19 AUGUST

My bags are packed for another week away. Today racing was at Worcester, where I rode two losers before going on down to Lambourn. In the morning I shall be doing some schooling for Nicky Henderson, and I'm looking forward to seeing how his good horses are coming along.

TUESDAY 20 AUGUST

Comparing Nicky's horses with John Jenkins' right now is like comparing a broodmare with a greyhound. John has a team specifically prepared for this time of year but Nick is content to wait, maybe impatiently, for the good ground. I did, however, school an experienced and successful American import called Running Comment, who will be out soon. I have high hopes of him, having been in the States with the British team last year when 'Franc' won a chase on him very comfortably.

WEDNESDAY 21 AUGUST

Drove down to Devon fearing I might fall asleep on my way to the start. My bedroom at the Francomes' house is directly above the piano room, in which John has a habit of playing at very odd times of day and night. It was 5.00 a.m. when he started tinkling today, just when I needed another few hours kip.

I managed to stay awake for my one ride, which was just as

well as things turned out. It was pouring with rain — again — and my horse Aboushabun seemed to take offence. He was in front coming to the water jump near the stands when suddenly he ducked out. There was nothing whatever I could do as he veered off, crashing through the rail, snapping the plastic as if it were a matchstick. The bottom of my boot hit the rail, taking the heel off, and if I had been riding three inches longer, I have no doubt that it would have taken my foot off instead. I didn't give it much thought at the time, but this evening, lying in my bath at The Palace, a shiver crept up my spine when I reflected on what might have been.

THURSDAY 22 AUGUST
Hywel Davies rode two winners today, breaking his duck for the season, and the broad smile on his face was one of undisguised relief. Hywel, the Welshman who won the Grand National in April, is another of whom the public have high expectations this term and, always an intense man, he had worn a permanently worried frown as that elusive winner refused to arrive for almost three weeks. It is a mental barrier as much as anything, and I am sure he will ride in more relaxed fashion from now on.

FRIDAY 23 AUGUST
The *Sporting Life* is on strike, a calamity for everyone involved in racing. Jockeys, especially, survive and organise their lives by knowing the four-day declarations for imminent meetings, and the *Life* is the only national paper which publishes them. It is not so bad at this time of year, when there is seldom more than one meeting each day anyway, but when there are two, three or even four possible venues to ride at on any one day, rides can take some sorting out. Seldom have I been so anxious for swift arbitration in any industrial dispute.

SATURDAY 24 AUGUST
For any freelance, the unwritten law is 'never turn down work'. But there are times when common-sense prevails. Today I had the choice of a six-hour round trip to Hereford for one ride on a

no-hoper, or a leisurely Saturday off, catching up on some sleep. No prizes for guessing my decision.

MONDAY 26 AUGUST

Pressure on a jockey is automatically increased when he knows that his horse's connections have had a punt. If you get beaten on one that is really fancied you know there will be no pats on the back when you return to unsaddle. Sometimes, however, the reaction is not at all what you expect. Take today. I rode a four-year-old called Taraius for John Jenkins. He had run in last season's Triumph Hurdle, and so should have outclassed everything in a Newton Abbot novice hurdle: the owners backed him to 4-6 and, knowing that, I threw everything in to try and get the horse's head in front. I failed, finished second — and, to my surprise, came back to be told by the trainer that I had been too hard on the horse!

THURSDAY 29 AUGUST

Had a haircut today, which was quite an achievement. It is such menial things, which other people take for granted, that I find so hard to fit in during the season. I have to book three days in advance with my hairdresser, and invariably I end up cancelling the appointment when an unexpected ride turns up.

My three days in Devon were not a great success; indeed, they were an irritation. I lost a couple of expected rides to Jonjo O'Neill, whom John Jenkins summoned from deepest Cumbria. They both got beaten — for which Jonjo was certainly not to blame — but John is well aware that I am unhappy at the situation. So far, I am biting my tongue.

FRIDAY 30 AUGUST

Gavin has a nice three-year-old called Boom Patrol. I schooled him for the first time today, just gently popping him over some hay-bales in Gavin's indoor school, and I was impressed. You will hear a lot more of the animal.

Schooling young horses is very satisfying to me. I did my apprenticeship with a fine trainer, Tom Jones, who taught me the proper method of schooling, step-by-step, and when I am called upon by any of my trainers I like to make sure things are done the right way. A horse's first school over obstacles is the most important. You need a decent lead horse who behaves impeccably, and you do not want the young horse to be frightened by what he is doing. If he is, and he carries that fear onto the racecourse when he first runs in a hurdle race, he could be ruined for a very long time. I have known trainers whose idea of schooling is to rush a novice across a couple of full-size hurdles, probably clattering through them both, and then send him to the races, where they cannot understand it when their charge runs as if he is scared and bewildered.

SATURDAY 31 AUGUST

That six-hour round-trip to Hereford confronted me again, but this time I had a feeling it would be worthwhile. Nicky Henderson's first runner of the term was the American horse, Running Comment, and although he was no more than half-fit, he trotted up. On firm ground at either end of the season, he will be a real force.

If Nicky was smiling, his Lambourn neighbour and mentor Fred Winter was not. Fred also had his first runners: both started favourite but one jumped awfully, losing all chance, and the other ran out. It's a great leveller, this game.

SEPTEMBER

SUNDAY 1 SEPTEMBER

At various stages of the season, and usually on a Sunday, I make a habit of sitting quietly in my own snug — a retreat from the world — and taking stock of what has passed. Today I looked back on August and concluded that it was a very satisfactory first month of the season. I am riding well, I am full of confidence and I have so far clocked up seven winners. That puts me second in the table behind John Jenkins' other jockey Simon Sherwood, but the gap is small. No one has broken away from the pack as John Francome did last season. There is still all to play for.

MONDAY 2 SEPTEMBER

Back to international business today. The British team of three — Peter Scudamore, Hywel Davies and myself — are taking on Ireland and France in a three-leg challenge match sponsored by the Irish-based pen manufacturers A.T. Cross. This was the opening leg in Galway, and in many ways it was typically Irish. There were a lot of non-runners, some chaotic moments in the presentation ceremonies and a good deal of the customary Irish 'it'll be all right on the night' outlook.

For us, it *was* all right, Britain taking a decent lead into the next leg, which is in France in three weeks time. We had arrived at Shannon airport by private plane, and three cars had been sent from Galway to ferry us to the racecourse. Jonjo O'Neill, (riding for Ireland on this occasion) Hywel and I were billetted with a man named Paul who had a fast car he insisted on driving at about 20 mph. I kept telling him to take off the handbrake but it made no difference, so we decided between us that there would be a change of driver on the return trip. I took the wheel, initially to Paul's obvious apprehension and later to his utter alarm. He sat in the back seat with his eyes closed, frequently crossing himself, and I have never seen such relief on a man's face as I saw on Paul's when we arrived at Shannon in about half the time it had taken us on the outward journey.

There was more fun to come. Back at Birmingham airport after a suitable amount of celebrating on board, there was a longish walk along concourses and down escalators to the customs desk. Finding an unused wheelchair was a temptation impossible for me to resist, and our manager David Nicholson did not take much persuading to sit in it, while I pushed him at considerable speed, scattering all in our path. Now, David — commonly known as 'The Duke' — has his critics for his superficial domineering manner. He frightens people, but under it all he is soft and, having ridden for him often, I know he is game for a laugh. On this occasion, however, he got rather more than he bargained for. The escalator loomed up quicker than I had expected and the pilot of our wheelchair, yours truly, opted to bail out, while D. Nicholson, still seated with his head hunched inside his coat, toppled onto the moving steps and, somehow, stayed intact to make one of the more unusual entrances this particular customs team can ever have seen.

TUESDAY 3 SEPTEMBER

When you are down in this game, life tends to kick you in the teeth. The current case of Mark Perrett proves my point. A year ago, Mark was riding a lot of winners in good style and people were speaking of him in glowing terms as a star of the future. Then he fell out with Stan Mellor, the trainer who retained him, and suddenly he was effectively 'out on the street'. Hugh O'Neill, a middle-of-the-road Surrey trainer, offered him his rides, and no sooner had he got going than Mark broke his leg. I heard the news today when Hugh phoned up to book me for one of his horses. I accepted with no particular pleasure.

THURSDAY 5 SEPTEMBER

The season is not yet six weeks old and Jonjo O'Neill has just suffered his second bad injury. This time it is a broken wrist — and he did not even do it on a racecourse, but in schooling. I am beginning to think Jonjo must have brittle bones, because every time he has a heavy fall he seems to break something. I do not, however, go along with the view that he wants to pack up riding or that he should. He has certainly not lost his nerve, which is the all-important thing; like most of us who have been around a few years he refrains from the unnecessary risks we might have taken as kids, but he still rides as hard as ever. He also still sees it all the same way I do — as being paid pretty well for doing something enjoyable. The day he stops is the day his problems begin to mount up. I hope he is not out for long.

SATURDAY 7 SEPTEMBER
Anthony Webber is an enigma. Even he would not claim to be the most stylish or rhythmical jockey around, but however much one might criticise him, the fact remains that horses do run for him. Today at Stratford he rode the winner of the novice chase, a horse of his father's called Ayle Hero. It was impossible to fault the ride he gave his horse until after jumping the last. Then, instead of coming across towards the inside rail to keep a course towards the post, he seemed to lose his sense of direction, carrying straight on towards the water-jump. I was chasing him in second place and could see this happening, so I stoked up my horse, knowing that Anthony would have to take a smart left turn to avoid the water and might be thought to have impeded me if I could get close enough. He saw the danger just in time and veered left, but I wasn't quite within striking distance and I had to be content with second place and a spot of ribbing at Anthony's expense.

WEDNESDAY 11 SEPTEMBER
First racing since Saturday. Rode in a novice chase at Fontwell, a hilly track where the downhill fences take prisoners at every meeting. Caution and commonsense is demanded, especially in the game of Russian Roulette, which is very often the closest thing to a novice chase. Yet today there were jockeys urging bad horses down that hill at a crazy, neckbreaking speed. I shouted to

one such lunatic to take it steady, but he took no notice. I passed him at the next fence — he was lying on the deck — and completed the race, grateful to be in one piece.

I have some sympathy with these jockeys though. In almost every case they are struggling riders who have to grab every opportunity and ride each horse they get on as if their life depends on it. But in giving everything, they take commitment to a dangerous degree at which they are risking serious injury to themselves and also putting the health of other riders at risk.

THURSDAY 12 SEPTEMBER

I am lying alone in bed at the Palace, Torquay. I feel I want to be sick, but I can't. Every bone in my body aches and I am honestly not sure which day of the week it is anymore — and all because I took a spare ride in a fillies' hurdle race at Newton Abbot.

It wasn't as if it looked a risky ride. The horse, Joscilla, was trained by Les Kennard and went off a warm favourite. But we got no further than the sixth hurdle before the horse ploughed straight into the obstacle and fired me into the firm autumn ground. I don't remember much more. The doctor probably should have signed me off for the compulsory seven-day period stipulated for concussion. Somehow I escaped. But God knows how many brain cells I killed with that fall. I must sleep . . . .

FRIDAY 13 SEPTEMBER

A suitable date for the way I feel. Getting out of bed was a monumental effort, and I felt as if I had been run over by a steamroller until an hour's soaking in a hot bath got rid of a certain amount of the stiffness.

The last thing I felt like doing was riding, but somehow I got through my one booked ride. Unfortunately it was the first race on the card, which gave me far too much time in the bar. Whisky can be an effective painkiller, I kept telling myself, but things did get out of hand, and for some reason I ended the evening in the bar of the Grand Atlantic Hotel, Weston-super-Mare!

SATURDAY 14 SEPTEMBER

This promised to be a good day, but it didn't turn out that way. It was the day on which John Francome was to have his first runner over jumps since taking up training — and I had the ride. The horse was Crimson Knight, and I use the word 'was' advisedly, because tonight Crimson Knight is dead and instead of celebrating an immediate success for one of my closest friends I am sharing in a nightmare.

I was on a high for 'Franc's' race, having just won the novice chase. I had taken the mickey out of John for bringing in his colours in a plastic shopping bag instead of the smart leather bags most trainers use, and I was enjoying the new experience of having him give me riding instructions in the paddock.

The horse was fancied, and with good reason. Turning for home, I challenged for the lead with Crimson Knight cruising. The moment he hit the front he found another gear, and he was running away from the pack as we approached the third-last hurdle. He met it on a long stride but instead of taking off, he stepped into the hurdle and we came down. What could I have done? Even as I lay on the grass I asked the question. But there was no good answer. When you have hit the front and you're flying, instinct insists you go for the long one if it's there. But this did not help the way I felt. John had ridden his first and his 1000th winners at Worcester and I had had the chance to give him his first training success there.

It made things much worse when word reached me later in the afternoon that the horse had dropped dead in his box, some time after the race. John had already left the course; someone would have to tell him on the phone. Knowing his phlegmatic approach, I guessed he would take it in his stride, but even if he did not feel upset, I did. Tonight I felt so low I didn't want to talk, drink or eat.

MONDAY 16 SEPTEMBER
Up at six o'clock to ride out for Alan Jarvis, who trains at Royston, only a short drive from Newmarket. He had told me yesterday that the ground was too firm for him to school any horses, but I decided to go anyway. Putting myself around like this, turning up to school or ride work at each of my trainers in turn, is a way of securing rides once their horses do run.

Alan Jarvis offered me a £10,000 retainer a few years ago and got as far as paying me the first instalment. It was big money then — probably the biggest sum ever offered to a jump jockey — but for various reasons we drifted apart before the middle of the season. Despite the inevitable gossip, there was no bad feeling between us; indeed, I like the guy a lot, and I look forward to riding his very good two-mile chaser Kathies Lad again this season.

TUESDAY 17 SEPTEMBER
Ever since that fall at Newton Abbot I've been suffering from bad headaches. The three days off at the start of this week would normally have been a frustration, just as the season has begun to get going, but the way I feel right now, they are very welcome.

WEDNESDAY 18 SEPTEMBER
I phoned Jonjo and Mark Perrett to try and cheer them up. Jonjo is his usual bouncy self and will be back in the saddle before too long, I expect. But Mark was depressed and in a lot of pain. He also said I was the first jockey to phone him in the two weeks since his fall. I'm afraid that does not say much for my profession.

THURSDAY 19 SEPTEMBER
My day began at 5.15 a.m. when I set off to school in Lambourn. Then it was on to open a shop for a friend in Street, Somerset, before riding at nearby Wincanton. Yet another fall — my third in the last five rides — which will do nothing for my head. Bought fish and chips on the way home. There is quite an art, I have discovered, to eating them while driving at 90 mph.

FRIDAY 20 SEPTEMBER
Huntingdon is my favourite course, partly because it is my most local track but also because it holds so many good memories. I had my first ride there, and my first 'chase winner. I've been leading jockey there for the past six or seven years, and I know the track so well that I have won races there that I had no right to. Having said all that, I logged a bad memory onto the Huntingdon file today when I turned up to ride Tamertown Lad for John

Jenkins and found that I had been 'jocked off'. John backed off when I had a go at him, saying that it was not his fault, and that the decision had been taken by the owners. But I remained upset, not just by the fact that Graham Bradley rode the horse and won, but that nobody had told me I was not required until I reached the course. As it was Huntingdon, I had only a short, sulky trip home, but what if it had been Wincanton? Would I still have received the same treatment?

SATURDAY 21 SEPTEMBER

A long weekend away, on team duties, began today. After racing at Warwick where I drew a blank, I joined up with the British and Irish teams to fly by private plane to Rennes in France for tomorrow's second leg of the A.T. Cross International. Then on Monday and Tuesday, in the unlikely settings of Plumpton and Sedgefield, I am in the South team for a match against the North. I have my doubts whether this event will work.

It turned out to be a long day. The Irish were late into Birmingham, so our plane was late arriving at Rennes. Then we had a long drive to Laval, and a hotel near the racecourse. We did not arrive until past midnight and I went straight to bed.

SUNDAY 22 SEPTEMBER

Last year we raced against the French in Paris. This is a bit of a contrast. Laval is a sleepy old market-town, as I discovered when I took a stroll before breakfast this morning. Considering that, the crowd at the races was enormous — almost 20,000 apparently — and it is easy to see why they brought the match here.

The French idea of a steeplechase is very different from ours. In England, the fences are uniform, with slight variations such as the open ditch and the water; in France, you race over all shapes, and sizes, including stone walls and steep banks. That in itself would have made things tricky, but the course also followed a complicated route and when Tony Mullins, the engagingly voluble one in the Irish team, announced that he would make the pace, I feared trouble. Sure enough, Tony was still ahead when he went the wrong way in mid-race and found himself disqualified. It might make a big difference — Frank Berry won the race for

34

Ireland, but we picked up plenty of place points and still have a healthy lead going into the last leg at Chepstow. The French, I'm afraid, are tailed off.

Another long day ended with a flight to Gatwick and a car transfer down to Brighton, where we will be spending the next two nights. Summoning some energy reserves I quizzed the hotel receptionist about the best night-clubs to patronise. 'It's Sunday,' she replied sullenly. 'They are all closed.' They would be, wouldn't they.

MONDAY 23 SEPTEMBER

My prediction about the North v South match proving a failure very nearly came true in the most unfortunate way. There were two match races at Plumpton today, and 15 minutes before the first of them was due 'off', the northern jockeys had still not arrived. I can't remember ever seeing so many worried faces on a racecourse before, nor so much relief when Graham Bradley, Phil Tuck, Chris Grant and Colin Hawkins sprinted breathlessly into the weighing-room even as the stewards were meeting to decide what action to take. I don't think many if any spectators in the surprisingly big crowd had any inkling of the panic, which was just as well.

'Brad' has always been a cool customer. He told me the saga of the boys missing a train connection in London and getting a cab all the way to the course, not daring to stop and ring up for fear of losing vital minutes. Then he went out and rode a well-judged race to win the first event. Sam Morshead won the next for us and our place points give us a ten-point advantage.

Tonight, I decided, Brighton would know I was in town. After a good fish meal attended by the eight jockeys in the match, Colin Hawkins and I set off in search of a night-spot. We were not discouraged by the obvious number of gays on the seafront, nor even by first impressions of the Brighton Belle Club. It was only after a drink and a look around that we realised we were conspicuous. Of all the men in the club, we were the only whites!

TUESDAY 24 SEPTEMBER

Sedgefield is a strange place. The course is in the middle of

35

nowhere and, from the riding viewpoint, there is a lot wrong with it. But somehow it is always well-patronised and today's event helped draw their biggest crowd in years. So I was wrong. The match worked; people came to watch, appeared to enjoy what they saw and everyone wants to do it again next year. That is fine by me. I love riding in team events — especially when we win, as happened today — and the great thing about this competition is that, on two difficult tracks, there were no problems in any of the four races because all eight of the competing jockeys were experienced and skilful. It makes so much difference.

WEDNESDAY 25 SEPTEMBER

Jamie Bouchard, a jockey mate of mine from a few years back, turned up at Devon today, soon after I had won the novice chase on Aboushabun. He has been in America for some time, and it is strange how seeing a face from the past can immediately conjure up the vivid image of a half-forgotten experience. In this case, Jamie Bouchard reminds me of the day I broke my neck.

Oddly enough, it was at Devon and Exeter that it happened. The Grand National was just eight days away and I recall having some attractive booked rides at Newbury the day after the Devon meeting. I had gone down to ride one for Ian Wardle in the handicap hurdle, and long before the business end of the race, I realised I had no chance. Approaching the last flight, I noticed that there was a gap in the hurdle, where one of the leaders had flattened it. I did the natural thing, steering my beaten horse through the gap rather than trying to jump it but, freakishly, he tripped on the fallen piece of brush and catapulted me out of the plate. The first thing to hit the ground was my head and the first thing I felt was a shock-wave shooting up my arm. This I thought, was nothing trivial.

A jockey's self-defence mechanisms demand that he should pretend he is not badly hurt, no matter how severe the fall or agonising the pain, and in the doctor's room I persuaded everyone who asked that I had done no more than twist my shoulder. In my heart I knew it was more serious — but I wanted to take those rides at Newbury the next day. I asked Jamie to phone up a physio in Hungerford the jockeys always use, and he managed to make me an appointment for later that evening. Jamie then put me in his car and we set off, after I had swallowed a couple of painkilling pills.

The pain hit me, half-an-hour up the motorway. The tablets had no further effect. I was in agony, and I told Jamie, with some reluctance, that there was no point in stopping at Hungerford, I just had to get home. Like the good friend he was, he drove me all the way to Newmarket, where I slept through an uncomfortable night before seeing a specialist the next morning.

He took x-rays and sent me back to bed, and it was late afternoon when he phoned and asked how I felt. 'Not good,' I replied. 'In fact, bloody awful.' 'I'm not at all surprised,' he said. 'You've broken your neck.' I didn't believe him at first. I had always thought that if you broke your neck, that was it — paralysis, wheelchair, end of career — but he explained that my spinal cord had remained intact with one vertebrae fractured and two others displaced. The ambulance, he added, was on its way.

The sequel to the story is quite uncanny. Exactly 12 months later I was riding in the same handicap hurdle on the same Devon card. Coming to the last, again with no chance, I saw there was a gap in that very same hurdle. If it is true that your whole life can flash before you, mine did in that moment. Quite what the trainer of my horse thought, let alone the spectators, I prefer not to know, but I yanked the horse's head back as hard as I could and pulled him up. Nothing in the world could have persuaded me to try and cross that hurdle, much less negotiate that gap.

THURSDAY 26 SEPTEMBER
One of my perennial problems is that I tend to dislocate my right knee if I fall heavily on it. It causes agony while it is out but I can put it back myself, leaving only a stiffness for the next day or so. It happened today at Uttoxeter. I had already ridden one winner, and looked as if I might ride another on the horse which fell. When I gave up my final ride, that won too!

On the way home I stopped off to see my parents. They have always lived in the Derbyshire village of Pinxton. It is a mining community and my Dad, Stan, was down the pit from the age of 14, until he retired quite recently. It had always been traditional in our village that the sons followed the fathers into the mine, but I don't think Dad would have let me, even if I had wanted to. Fortunately, the thought never crossed my mind.

FRIDAY 27 SEPTEMBER

The years might be catching up with me. I was suffering today, riding in the heat, and I wonder if I can go on burning the candle at both ends. It is not, however, affecting my riding, and I scored my third novice chase winner in successive days on Celtic Story. I've always said that novice chases sort out the men from the boys!

SATURDAY 28 SEPTEMBER

On Thursday I came across a young claiming rider named Ricky Balfour. I'd neither heard of him nor seen him ride before, and I left Uttoxeter not caring whether I ever did again after a reckless piece of riding in the novice chase which could have caused chaos. Today, just my luck, I was up against him in another chase, and he followed his Uttoxeter tactics of setting off at a lunatic pace and trying to make all, never giving his horse a chance to recover from mistakes but winding him up and slinging him into the next fence. I kept my wits about me behind him, which was just as well, as he careered through the wing of a fence half-way round, and nearly took two more with him. He also rode in the novice chase, and I watched him knocking spots off a no-hoper at the back of the field. It was a sad sight. I understand that the lad does not get many rides and wants to make an impression, but he is going the wrong way about it.

OCTOBER

TUESDAY 1 OCTOBER
I've been feeling lousy lately and can't decide why. It's nothing specific, I'm just not bouncing and bubbling as I should be. So today I had an appointment in London with Dr Michael Allen, the Jockey Club's chief medical officer. He gave me a thorough check and, late this evening, telephoned me at home to tell me that my chest x-rays were clear. This was a big relief. When you are feeling rough it is, I suppose, natural to fear the worst and although the doctor has not immediately been able to tell me what *is* wrong, he has been able to reassure me about what is not wrong.

WEDNESDAY 2 OCTOBER
By this time of year I'm usually sparking, eager to go anywhere for a potential winner. But my state of mind was summed up today when I had to drag my reluctant self to Ludlow for one ride. It is a three-hour-plus drive to Ludlow and by the time I got there I was wishing I hadn't bothered. But I got down to concentrating on the race in hand, and decided that my horse, Balmatt, had only a notorious runner-up called Karnatak to beat. I chose to track Karnatak until the last possible moment and then, trusting his reputation as a reluctant finisher, try to beat him for toe after the last. It worked to perfection and I passed him ten yards from the line to win. The best-laid and most sensible plans often come to nothing in the hurly-burly of a race but it is a nice feeling when one does work. The drive home seemed a lot sweeter and quicker.

THURSDAY 3 OCTOBER

John Jenkins had booked me for one ride at Fontwell on a horse called First Temptation. He warned me it was a small horse and he wasn't wrong ... I've seen bigger rabbits. But the man knows how to train them — he won by half-a-length and another long drive was justified.

Got home late and a glance at the results told me that 'Sharky' Sherwood has ridden another winner. Every time I get one, he replies, and he is still a few up on me.

FRIDAY 4 OCTOBER

I've seen everything now. The first event at Hereford today was a hurdle race with only three runners. The favourite ran out when clear, his market rival took it up, but then fell to leave the outsider to come home alone. But Robin Dickin, the jockey of the faller, remounted with what turned out to be a broken collarbone. He finished all right, though what further damage he might have done I can't imagine. For this piece of extraordinary bravado his percentage of the place money works out at a princely £4.50!

Newmarket to Hereford is 166 miles, and I did a spot of wally-watching. I noticed that around 90 per cent of the idiots who accelerate while you are overtaking them, or cut you up on roundabouts, have beards. If you come across one sporting a beard *and* glasses, you are in big trouble.

SATURDAY 5 OCTOBER

A landmark in every jumping season is the first televised meeting. For me, this always means reminding myself to curb my bad language down at the start. Whenever I watch TV videos the boom mike always seems to pick out my voice uttering some expletive as the starter calls us into line. My mother does not approve!

It was Chepstow who hosted the cameras today and an additional attraction was the finale of the A.T. Cross International. We came into this last leg with a decent lead and I looked like putting the result beyond doubt when, in the first of the remaining two races, I sent my mount Yacare into a clear lead on the run-in. But with the race won, he stuck his head in the air and tried to pull himself up. Rhythmic Pastimes, ridden by Ireland's Tommy Carmody, got up to beat me in a desperately close photograph. It was a horrible feeling, the race and the points slipping away like that — only made worse by the fact that the winner is normally my ride. Carmody also won the international chase, but we scrambled enough points to hang on and win the match.

MONDAY 7 OCTOBER
There are only four jump jockeys based in Newmarket — Simon McNeil, Jeff Barlow, Johnny McLaughlin and myself — and whenever we travel together, usually to a midweek midland meeting, a late night is guaranteed. It was Southwell today; all four of us were on parade and a pub-crawl back down the A1 meant I managed to get home at 3.00 a.m. Perhaps it's no wonder Jeff's wife threatens to divorce him every time I phone up to go racing with him!

WEDNESDAY 9 OCTOBER
I didn't have a ride at Cheltenham and I wasn't sorry — still not feeling right, and I slept all afternoon.

FRIDAY 11 OCTOBER
The schooling grounds at Lambourn are the scene of many a lost temper before breakfast and today, as I got down to schooling some of Nicky Henderson's young horses, I am afraid we added to the record of the place with a sizeable barney.

I have been brought up to believe that you should only school novices with an experienced lead horse. Nicky has different ideas, and we had no lead horse at all this morning. In my view it was the blind leading the blind, and the horses did not learn much. I said so, and Nicky said his piece in reply. He is the boss; he has to train the horses and answer to the owners. But I am not sorry I made the point, even if the atmosphere was frosty afterwards.

SATURDAY 12 OCTOBER
An unwelcoming day. The weather is still unseasonally warm, the ground unkindly firm, and all I had to cheer me was two moderate rides at Uttoxeter. The novice chase was full of amateurs and

41

conditional jockeys, and I felt quite the father figure down at the start. I loudly told everyone that I would lead them on Celtic Story, and when one lad came upsides me at the third fence I snarled and growled at him and he dutifully dropped back, never to be seen again. I got beaten by half-a-length but had no trouble in running.

SUNDAY 13 OCTOBER

Every jockey loses a ride now and then, but some hurt more than others. Gavin told me this morning that the owners of Work Mate were upset over the way I rode the horse at Southwell last Monday, and are insisting I don't ride him again. Fair enough, the horse was favourite and trailed in near the back, prompting an inevitable stewards' enquiry. But my explanation that the torrential rain had altered the going, and that Work Mate could not act on the soft, was accepted because it was the absolute truth. The owners appear to be suggesting something more devious, which particularly annoys me as I have devoted a lot of time and patience to their horse. Work Mate was never a natural jumper but I put in a lot of hours schooling him and, last season, he repaid the effort by winning two hurdles and a chase. And this is the thanks I get.

Oddly enough the same thing has happened to Peter Scudamore. He has been 'jocked off' Ace of Spies, a very useful horse on whom he has won two hurdle races. 'Scu' taught that horse everything about jumping, but after one disappointing race the owner has got rid of him. This can be a cruel job sometimes. I don't know about 'Scu', but I don't intend to bite my tongue when next I meet the owners of Work Mate.

TUESDAY 15 OCTOBER

Morning schooling sessions are a pleasure to me on days when I am not in a tearing rush to get to the races. I had no rides at Newton Abbot today so I popped a few of Di's horses over the obstacles. I'll be doing this a lot more for her when I finally pack up riding and I really enjoy seeing the horses improve as they learn.

The rain has arrived at last and it's pissing down. I built a big log-fire this afternoon and put my feet up.

WEDNESDAY 16 OCTOBER

I had never ridden for John Ffitch-Heyes before, but I knew of the man and I could even spell his name. It seems I was not quite so familiar to him, however. He phoned me last night to ride a couple for him at Plumpton today but I was bewildered when I answered the call and he asked for 'Stan'. 'Who?' I replied. 'Stan Smith Eccles' he repeated — and I could tell he wasn't joking. Still, I've only been riding 15 years. I can't expect people to know my name yet, can I!?

My other ride was for Philip Mitchell, a headstrong horse called Eurolink Boy I had happened to draw in the North v South match last month. As I finished third on him I kept the ride — but today was different. Today was his first time over fences, and I'm not likely to forget it. He stuck his head in the air going to the first, and I quickly realised that there was no way I could stop him. He dived through the fence, somehow keeping his balance and his rider at the other side, and then steamed down that sharp Plumpton hill as if we were in a five-furlong sprint. He met the downhill fences well, more by luck than judgement I would say, but by now I freely admit I was *frightened*. There is a railway station at the bottom of the Plumpton hill, well-used by the punters who flock down to this pleasant little Sussex course from 'the smoke'. I had serious doubts whether we would negotiate the turn before the station and had a momentary vision of leaping the rails onto platform two.

Alarming though he is, however, he is not that bad a horse. He turned the bend all right and then I had him under control. Up past the stands I kept a tight hold on him, and as we turned down the hill for the last time I was ten lengths second. Loose horses were darting in and out, making life even more hazardous, but I let my animal go again and he responded, joining the leader after the second last and going away to win. I think I can say I earned my percentage of this one!

THURSDAY 17 OCTOBER

Sometimes, being popular has its drawbacks. My phone has been red-hot today with two trainers blowing their top at me on the subject of one three-year-old hurdle at Market Rasen tomorrow.

Patrick Haslam, who trains in Newmarket, had asked me to ride Armorad for him. I had been up to school the horse, I knew he was fancied and I took the booking early in the week after putting in a precautionary call to John Jenkins to see if he was likely to run any of his in the race. The answer was initially negative, but then John phoned this morning to say he wanted me to ride one for him after all. In a situation like this a jockey cannot win. I phoned Patrick to try and get off Armorad and he was furious. I phoned John again to tell him I wasn't available and *he* was furious. I eventually opted to ride Armorad on the freelance basis of first come, first served. But it was not a happy decision.

FRIDAY 18 OCTOBER
Armorad got beaten. It had to happen after the rows of yesterday, and the only relief was that the Jenkins horse did not win either.

I drowned my sorrows on the way home with two of the Newmarket Musketeers, Messrs Barlow and McLaughlin. The 90-minute journey took us eight hours!

SATURDAY 19 OCTOBER
The day began with that warm glow of anticipation a jockey gets when he has a full book of decent rides on a major card. It ended with a feeling of utter deflation.

It was Kempton, the first London meeting of the season and the best-class programme seen anywhere to date. I rode Running Comment, Rhythmic Pastimes, Duke of Milan, Hot Match and Billion Boy — all previous winners and all with some sort of chance. It was a mouthwatering prospect and I set off early to avoid the crowds and ensure I had time for a game of pool in the plush new Kempton weighing-room complex which now makes it such a popular venue among the jockeys. On the drive down the M11 and across the north of London I weighed up my prospects for the afternoon and concluded it was the sort of day on which I ought to have one winner, might well have two, and could conceivably have even more.

I had none. It was gloriously sunny weather, there was a large crowd and the atmosphere was perfect. But I got beaten on everything, including three favourites. Two seconds and a third was the sum total of my efforts and I drove home in a mood diametrically opposed to the sunny enthusiasm of my outward journey just a few hours earlier.

SUNDAY 20 OCTOBER
I am too fed up for even the usual Sunday routine of ringing round my regular trainers. Yesterday was a big disappointment and, although there were excuses for the defeat of each of the five I rode, it was still a bitter pill to swallow after waking up to a day of such promise.

I cheered myself up this evening with my regular Sunday programme: 6.00p.m. switch on Channel Four for the American football; 7.30p.m. drive to the Willie Thorne Snooker Centre in Newmarket. If I hadn't been a jockey I think I would like to have played American football, and I never miss my Sunday night diet of quarterbacks and first-downs. As for snooker, well, I'm improving and I enjoy it.

MONDAY 21 OCTOBER
No jump racing in Britain today. None of us objects to the occasional free day but I am baffled by the logic of the race-planners at the Jockey Club. Take last week, for instance — again, Monday was a complete blank, yet on Wednesday there were meetings at Plumpton, Towcester and Wetherby. Surely it would have made more sense to run one of the three on the Monday?

I drove to London tonight for a British team reception hosted by Austin Reed of Regent Street. They have kitted out the jockeys' team in a uniform of blazer, slacks and tie, and it is striking just what an impression we create when travelling abroad through the fact that we *look* like a team.

TUESDAY 22 OCTOBER
Oh dear, more bad news. Gavin phoned this morning and said somewhat ominously that he'd like to see me. I drove down to his yard and he broke the news that another one of his owners has complained about my riding. This time the horse concerned is

45

Hot Match, who finished last of four at Kempton on Saturday. The owner was not pleased with the way I rode him and wants someone else. I believe the horse is badly handicapped at present, and at Kempton he was giving lumps of weight to the other three, coming up against a horse called Peter Anthony who is a real flier on fast ground. Not surprisingly, Hot Match couldn't go the pace and was well beaten. I did not think his defeat had anything to do with my riding. Fortunately, Gavin agrees. He has told the owner concerned that I am his jockey and he will continue to put me up on his horse. So now the ball is back in the owner's court. I appreciate Gavin sticking by me, but this is certainly turning into a few days I will be keen to forget.

WEDNESDAY 23 OCTOBER

The arrangement with John Jenkins is not working out quite as I had hoped. In fact it is increasingly clear that Simon Sherwood is getting most of the Jenkins' rides, which is why he is some way ahead of me at the top of the jockeys' table. He rode another winner for John at Cheltenham today and is riding with a great deal of style and confidence. I'm pleased for him, if disappointed for myself, but as regards the championship I must say I currently fear Hywel Davies the most. He is in third place, but his main retainer Tim Forster has hardly run any of his stars yet, and it will be a formidable stable once they get going.

THURSDAY 24 OCTOBER

This was a day off with a difference — no rides, no food and virtually nothing to drink. With two meetings on it's very frustrating to be sat at home, but the ground is still hard and spare rides are like gold-dust. Tomorrow, however, it is Newbury — the first jumping of the term on one of my favourite courses — and I ride Dhofar for Gavin in a handicap hurdle. He is well weighted with only 10-2, and Gavin has warned me he does not expect any overweight. So this morning, after a cup of tea and a slice of toast, I took two de-appetiser pills and resigned myself to eating nothing more before the race.

I take these tablets because I hate saunas and I have no willpower to control my eating voluntarily. They certainly work, in

46

that I rapidly lose all urge to eat, but their side-effects are not pleasant. They make me feel tense and nervous and I find it hard to sleep when I've taken them — I lie awake with my brain racing. I only hope it's worth it. Putting up overweight creates a poor impression and is rightly considered unprofessional if your horse is at all fancied. But the effort and sacrifices demanded to lose the necessary pounds can seem painfully futile if the end result is a mention in the *Sporting Life* reading 'tailed off', 'never dangerous' or — perhaps the most frustrating of all — 'caught on line'.

FRIDAY 25 OCTOBER

Dhofar was far from tailed off and, although at the final flight there seemed a danger he might be caught on the line, he sprinted away again to make the wasting worthwhile and give yours truly something extra to celebrate: my 500th winner. I had done my homework about this race, and a snap poll of the other jockeys in the weighing-room confirmed my fears that no one wanted to make the running and give my horse the strong gallop he needs over two miles. So, in the parade ring, I told Gavin we had no choice but to make the running ourselves — and we did exactly that, knocking three seconds off the Newbury two-mile record in the process. Another plan which worked!

Dhofar was my second win of the day, but the horse which broke a worrying barren run stretching back three weeks and a day was Kings Bridge. Off-course punters, I hear, were surprised to see that I rode this horse. I have news for them all — so was I. The horse is owned by Freddie Starr and trained by John Jenkins. I had phoned John last night to ask him if he ran Rhythmic Pastimes on Saturday. He said he didn't and mentioned nothing about any other possible rides, so I rang off. Imagine my surprise when the phone rang at seven o'clock this morning and John asked me to ride Kings Bridge in the first at Newbury today!

Kings Bridge, I discovered, had useful form in Ireland, but he was out of the handicap here and I had to put up a couple of pounds overweight. Even the de-appetiser pills did not enable me to ride at 10 stone. My first sight of the horse was far from encouraging — he is an ugly animal who looks as if he might recently have been released from pit duties. But as is his habit,

John had produced him fit and well, the horse jumped admirably and came through after the last to win, giving John his 40th winner of the season and bringing me a great deal of relief after an especially rough fortnight.

Completing 500 winners leaves me with one overwhelming emotion — total admiration for Stan Mellor and John Francome, the only men to have ridden twice that number. Right now, I cannot see myself lasting that long!

SATURDAY 26 OCTOBER

A Saturday meeting at my local course, Huntingdon, would normally guarantee me a healthy list of rides. Today, with no respite from the drought and the firm ground, I had only one — but it was an important one. Gavin had talked the owners of Hot Match round to his way of thinking and I was on board again. Once more, I thought the horse had too much weight with 11 stone 10 pounds, and once again he was outpaced. But second place was an improvement and everyone seemed much happier this time.

SUNDAY 27 OCTOBER

My phone calls brought the response from trainers I have come to expect: 'If it rains, we'll run some horses. If not, we will just go on waiting.' I would do and say exactly the same in their shoes, but I must say this Indian summer is dragging its feet and I'm about fed up with it.

I habitually complete all my phoning before lunch on a Sunday and tend to get very tetchy with anyone who bothers me afterwards. I regard Sunday afternoon and evening as my sacred free time and if I do pick up the phone — because I never take it off the hook — I am pretty short-tempered, making it very clear to callers that they should modify their telephoning times in future. People in racing — and I mean trainers as well as jockeys — are on duty most hours of the day, seven days a week, and I feel I am entitled to cut myself off from the job just for a short time each week.

MONDAY 28 OCTOBER

Fakenham is one of the charming eccentricities of the English jumping scene. Set just a few miles from the north Norfolk coast, the tip of a triangle with Kings Lynn and Norwich, it is part of a sleepy and ancient town and has attractions one would never associate with, shall we say, Ascot or Newbury. The only approach road, for instance, is riddled with stones, boulders and ruts to test any tyre or exhaust system. The grandstand, over 100 years old, looks quaint enough but it houses the weighing-room and I can relate from bitter experience that, on a December afternoon, there are many better places to be; the few, high windows steam up, the pipes and the walls attract condensation and the room becomes damp, uncomfortable and uncivilised.

Having said that, I am all for preserving the Fakenhams of the jumping world. You meet real people here, real jumping enthusiasts. Plenty of them speak with Norfolk accents I find it impossible to understand, but they love the game and this course is always well patronised. For some reason it also draws hordes of the green-wellies brigade, the Hoorah Henries and their Penelope and Samantha girlfriends. The ladies do the scenery no harm.

It was packed today. They don't race here often, and the locals like to make the most of their chances. So do a few trainers. Rex Carter, based just down the road in Swaffham, turned out three winners, while Philip Mitchell, who trains in Epsom but treats Fakenham like a favoured local course, had two. I didn't have any, but I still enjoyed the day, and in the wooden shack which passes for a bar, I stood with a whisky after the last race half listening to the strains of a Norfolk earbasher whose views I could neither understand nor enthuse over. It wouldn't happen at Ascot, I thought — but that doesn't necessarily make Ascot any the better.

TUESDAY 29 OCTOBER

I am trying to improve my golf. There is not much chance of playing the game regularly in this job, but on recent days off I've taken to spending the afternoons at the Newmarket course, investigating its ample rough. I play off 24 and rely on connecting lustily with the occasional drive, but if I had more free time to spend on the course, I think I could get quite attached to the game.

49

WEDNESDAY 30 OCTOBER

The drought must surely end soon. The Ascot meeting was televised today but there were only 25 runners on the entire card and I didn't ride one of them. Instead I sat at home in front of the TV, critically appraising the styles of my fellow jockeys, and secretly wishing I was out there with them.

THURSDAY 31 OCTOBER

A bad month ended on an appropriate note. I drove all the way to Wincanton for one ride on a horse with no logical chance, only to be told when I got there, a shade car-weary, that he was a non-runner. I drove on to spend the night in Torquay before tomorrow's Devon meeting and had plenty of time to reflect on the misfortunes of October. The score adds up to 28 rides, only five winners, a few rows with trainers and owners, and a general frustration that the season has still not properly got underway. Things can now only improve.

NOVEMBER

FRIDAY 1 NOVEMBER

Losing any race on an objection figures among the greatest irritations in a jockey's life. Whatever the justice of the verdict, the rider will invariably feel aggrieved as he has done his bit in getting his horse first past the post. All the effort is suddenly for nothing, and the deflation most acute, when the stewards reverse the placings. It is not often, however, that a horse is demoted after winning his race by as much as seven lengths, as happened to my mount Kings Bridge at Devon today.

This was the horse on which I had won a competitive 'chase at Newbury after being booked to ride, by John Jenkins, only on the morning of the race. This time things were a little different. The race had been mapped out for the horse and I was always going to ride him. We were also expected to win and the owner, Freddie Starr, was bubbling with wit and confidence before the off.

The race panned out into a two-horse finish. Over the final three fences I raced neck and neck with Brendan Powell, riding a prolific winner called My Bonnie Prince. I knew instinctively that all was not well with Kings Bridge as he began to go severely left-handed, and when I resorted to the whip after the last he ran away from it, veering across My Bonnie Prince. The interference was obvious, though accidental, and although by now I was convinced that Kings Bridge was lame, I roused him to run on again and we went away to win by that wide margin of seven lengths.

As soon as we passed the post I pulled the horse up and jumped off — the usual routine followed by a jockey who is aware he has a lame horse under him. I was expecting a steward's enquiry and had no immediate qualms when Brendan told me his owners wanted him to object. Having won by so far I thought I had a very reasonable chance of keeping the race. The stewards, however, viewed the video of the offending incident and decided otherwise. It was sickening for me, probably worse still for Freddie who likes nice trophies on his mantlepiece and had rather taken a fancy to this one. My day was not improved by my one other ride, also for John Jenkins, in the seller. I think I could have finished faster than my horse if I had got off and run.

SATURDAY 2 NOVEMBER

What a difference a day makes. Yesterday I had two disappointments, today two winners — and one of them came through the rare privilege of a walkover. With the going still very firm at Sandown, Rhythmic Pastimes was the only horse to stand his ground for a £3,000 novice chase and the only effort demanded of me was to don the correct colours, weigh out, mount, and canter down to the first fence and back. Not a difficult way to earn my riding fee, plus the ten per cent of the prize money. It was only the second walkover of my entire career.

I had to work rather harder on my other winner but as it was Duke of Milan I enjoyed every second. I couldn't settle him in as I had hoped to, because an amateur rider named Tom Grantham, riding Tom's Little Al, was on my withers all the way, but the 'Duke' jumped immaculately as ever and came right away to win comfortably, breaking the track record by all of three seconds.

Sandown has always been among my favourite tracks. I tend to do well here, which is a big factor, but I also consider it a fair and challenging course which happens to have just about the best facilities you could hope to find on an English racetrack.

If I thought I'd had a good day, however, Peter Scudamore had a far better one. He rode four winners on the other big card at Chepstow, all for his guv'nor David Nicholson. I was pleased for them both. 'The Duke's' stable had a disastrous time last season, suffering from some sort of virus, and I am quite sure 'Scu' was tapped up by other trainers, and perhaps even tempted to move. He loyally stayed on, however, and it seems he is now beginning to see some reward.

TUESDAY 5 NOVEMBER

No jockey likes to be unseated during a race. The difference between a horse falling and simply ejecting his rider, giving him no chance of staying in the plate, can be extremely slim, and we all accept that the occasional dreaded 'U' is inevitable in a chase. To be unseated over hurdles, however, is undignified and degrading. The first emotion of a jockey when this happens is usually embarrassment, though when I suffered the fate at Fontwell today I must say I first felt relief that I was unscathed as my mount had roguishly attempted to duck into the wing of the third last hurdle, which could have had very painful consequences for both of us. But after that, and on the long way back to the weighing-room, yes, I felt embarrassed.

I celebrated Guy Fawkes' night at Oliver Sherwood's Lambourn home. All the trainers in the village seemed to be around Oliver's bonfire and as the beverage on offer was a particularly potent mulled wine I have not for some while seen such a drunken gathering.

Racing folk tend towards the manic side of humour when off-duty and socialising. Tonight was no exception and the star turn during a variety show of misbehaviour was performed by trainer Nicky Vigors who drove a car straight through the blazing fire and leapt out on the other side howling with laughter. Amused but appalled, I remarked that he must be crazy, but he retorted: 'Not as crazy as you think ... it's not my car!'

WEDNESDAY 6 NOVEMBER

Fortified by the mulled wine, I won on both my rides at Newbury. I got a novice hurdler up on the line to win by a hard-fought neck but derived far more pleasure from victory on Rhythmic Pastimes in the novice chase. He had not jumped well early in his chasing debut and I had been easy on him, trying to teach him something and do little more than get him round safely. With that achieved, and a Sandown walkover in the bag, he took on Fulke Walwyn's highly-rated Arctic Stream today over two-and-a-half miles. A wide grin crossed my face when he met the first fence wrong but fiddled it expertly. He had learned a lot, and from then on he hardly put a foot wrong. He went round this testing track like an experienced handicapper and won on the bridle, beating Arctic Stream by 12 lengths, which might have been doubled if I had changed up a gear. It is a great feeling when a horse of obvious ability can be helped to make the difficult transition from hurdles to fences and then shows the benefit with a performance like this, and I drove home in high good humour.

THURSDAY 7 NOVEMBER
It is a golden rule of mine never to go racing when I don't have any rides. I don't believe it looks good, a jockey hanging around like an out-of-work actor at an opening night, and anyway I get very bored watching a meeting in which I have no involvement. But today I broke that rule and drove to Kempton for a business meeting. The business was conducted quickly enough and then I wished I was somewhere else. Restless and out of place, I left the course as quickly as was polite.

FRIDAY 8 NOVEMBER
Cheltenham's Mackeson meeting is regarded by most people in jumping as the launch of First Division National Hunt racing. The crowds roll up by tradition, the prize money is high and the Mackeson itself is, of course, an institution. Today was the first day of the meeting and here I was, a top jockey, sitting at home without a single ride. Frustration is one word for it . . . .

SATURDAY 9 NOVEMBER
My dejection at having no ride in the Mackeson was lifted by winning on Kumbi in a valuable long-distance chase later in the afternoon. I reckon Kumbi must be the biggest and strongest horse in training — he ploughed straight through the tricky downhill fence which accounts for so many, yet never even broke stride, and stayed on really well up the taxing final hill to give 'Ginger' McCain, a trainer I like enormously, his first Cheltenham winner in a long while. He and the horse's owner are already talking about taking Kumbi to Aintree for his third crack at the Grand National but, from my own point of view, I am far from convinced he is the sort of conveyance any right-minded jockey would wish to be on when jumping those awesome fences. On

park courses he can get away with his blunders, and an able pilot can stay on board. At Liverpool Kumbi may not fall, but he has already twice displayed a penchant for getting rid of his rider. I can hardly blame 'Ginger' for being keen, though. He trains in homely premises at Southport, Aintree being his local course, and it would be a dream come true for him if he could produce another National winner to follow in the legendary footsteps of his greatest horse Red Rum, who is still in his number one box now.

The afternoon belonged to Richard Linley, who won the Mackeson for the third time in four years, on Fred Winter's Half Free. But the evening was scheduled to belong to Fred's ex-jockey, one J. Francome, due to receive his seventh and last champion jockey's award at the annual ball staged in the banqueting rooms at Cheltenham. Unfortunately, John had made something of a cock-up. His memory for dates not being his greatest quality, he had some time ago accepted an invitation to host a celebrity sports forum in Birmingham tonight. Programmes had been printed, the Francome name had been freely touted as an inducement to potential ticket-buyers, and the organisers were understandably miffed when they phoned John a few days ago to make final arrangements and were informed that not only had he forgotten all about it but that he was also due at the ball. The Francome phone was apparently busy for some minutes after this revelation and the upshot was that his speech — which some of us have come to look forward to as much as the meal and the ball itself — was delivered, with a delicious disregard for convention, just before the soup course, whereupon the ever-controversial 'Franc' made his apologies and jumped into his Porsche (sadly a newer model than mine) to hotfoot it to Brum!

Typical John, he didn't leave us without a laugh. Sporting his usual deadpan face as he drawled his jokes, he told one about three trainers — Fred Winter, Mercy Rimell and David Nicholson — having an audience with God at which each was to be granted one wish. Fred asked if he could win the Gold Cup again before he died and, sure enough, God allowed him his ambition and even told him the year it would happen. Mrs Rimell's wish was to train another Champion Hurdler before she died. God granted this and revealed the relevant year. Then David who, remarkably, has never trained a winner at the Festival meeting, was called to make his request. He asked, not surprisingly, when he would be allowed to train a Cheltenham winner. 'Good gracious no,' replied God. '*I'll* be dead before that happens!'

SUNDAY 10 NOVEMBER
I had stayed overnight with Pete Scudamore and the drive back to Newmarket with a pounding head and all the hangover trimmings was a long and painful experience. On arrival, I abandoned plans to phone trainers — some of whom, I guessed, might be feeling just as rough — and went straight to bed.

MONDAY 11 NOVEMBER
Plumpton was the only southern meeting today and I had no booked rides. Catching up with the planning I should have done yesterday, I phoned John Jenkins at ten o'clock to ask him what I might ride for him during the rest of the week. He told me he would not be running much until the weekend but then, to my astonishment, he said: 'What are you doing today?' When I told him I had a day off, he said: 'Right, get yourself down to Plumpton and you can ride one for me in the last.'

I had noticed in the *Life* that he was due to run a novice hurdler which had no declared jockey, but had glibly assumed he must have booked someone else. With John, however, this should never be assumed. Amazed though I was to pick up a ride in such a casual manner, I packed my bags for the week and set off for Sussex. The horse ran promisingly and finished third so I did not consider it a wasted journey, and I drove back only as far as Lambourn, to spend the night with 'Franc'.

TUESDAY 12 NOVEMBER
Despite being dragged bodily from my bed to ride out for John and earn my usual generous breakfast, I was in good form this morning. One of the horses I have most been looking forward to partnering is Kathies Lad and he was to make his seasonal debut at Devon, in quite a valuable chase. He won, too, despite being only half-fit and not being given too hard a race. With luck, the

two of us can add further to last season's successes at Cheltenham and Aintree.

I spent the evening with Simon Sherwood, thus exploding the myth that rival sportsmen never socialise. Simon and I are actually good buddies, and will hopefully remain so whatever may befall us in the contest for this season's jockeys' title. Anyone who imagines us at daggers drawn would have been startled to observe us together in The Swan Inn at Shefford, near Lambourn, where the Sherwood brothers were celebrating today's win by one of their hurdlers, Atrabates, with the horse's owners. There appeared to be dozens of them, and it transpires they are all members of the Atrabates Cricket Club. They certainly know how to celebrate.

WEDNESDAY 13 NOVEMBER
Some day soon the rains will come. Then, I guess, it will teem down for a fortnight and we will all moan about it. Right now, however, everyone in racing is praying for some rain to ease one of the longest autumn droughts I can remember. Underfoot conditions are now so bad that today there were two walkovers on the Wolverhampton card — something I have never known before.

I was at Newbury for a single ride on Nick Henderson's Smart Reply. We quietly fancied him, but to no avail. He ran deplorably and I retired to The Five Bells, a welcoming pub between Newbury and Lambourn run by a charming and hospitable lady called Dottie Channing-Williams. It is among the favourite haunts of all racing people in this area, and deservedly so.

THURSDAY 14 NOVEMBER
Every experienced jockey knows that trying to sneak up the inside rail on a bend is a dangerous manoeuvre at the best of times, and can often be construed as asking for trouble. It is a common sight to see the 'door closed' by the man in front when he senses someone attempting this and, unbeknown to the crowd up in the stands, there is frequently a good deal of shouting and swearing between the jockeys involved. On some courses it is more hazardous than others. Wincanton, for instance, has a final bend on

57

which there is often trouble, and today Peter Scudamore and Graham McCourt had such a tussle, as Graham cheekily tried to slip up 'Scu's' inner that they conveniently left the race for me to win on a horse called Comedy Lane. Their argument, loud and angry on the course, resumed in the weighing-room where I feared for one moment that these two normally mild characters would come to blows. I kept out of the way and went out to ride another winner on Duke of Milan. To complete a highly satisfactory day, it is now raining hard.

FRIDAY 15 NOVEMBER

In 99 cases out of 100, a jockey involved in a photo-finish knows his fate. To the crowd it might seem well-nigh impossible to separate the horses, but a jockey has a sixth sense which tells him whether he is in front, or just behind, as the winning-post flashes past. I usually manage to look across at the post without interrupting my riding, and today, in a televised chase at Ascot, I was unhappily convinced that Richard Rowe on Paddyboro had touched me off in a desperately tight finish. I was riding Destiny Bay, a decent horse of Nicky Henderson's having his first run of the season; and I was so sure I had been beaten that I returned to the runners-up position in the winners' enclosure and was virtually back in the weighing-room when the announcement gave me the race and a mix of surprise and delight.

A winner on TV always gives a jockey a boost, and today I had two, which makes six winners in the last six racing days. Things are at last starting to happen after a sticky patch, but as usual, whenever you get up, something happens to knock you down.

I had been asked to go to Newcastle tomorrow. It is a hell of a journey, one I normally wouldn't relish at all, but as it was the David Steele-John Jenkins team who had booked me to ride their very good hurdler Wing and a Prayer, I had agreed. The race was a valuable one — the Fighting Fifth Hurdle — and I was also swayed by the hint that I was back in favour with Mr Steele who, despite the fact that I have ridden him a lot of winners, seemed to be reluctant to have me on his string of horses this season. So, although I had little chance of picking up any further rides in what is virtually foreign territory to a southern jockey, I was

58

looking forward to going. Imagine my surprise, then, when I arrived at Ascot at midday, asked my valet John Buckingham to lay out my tack after racing so that I could take it to Newcastle, only to have him tell me that I wouldn't be going. Wing and a Prayer had been pulled out of the race at the overnight stage and no one had thought to tell me. Having turned down a number of rides at Ascot, I have now had to scramble to get back on them. I've only been successful with one, Gavin's Boom Patrol, so my Saturday plans have to some extent been wrecked.

SATURDAY 16 NOVEMBER

We have to try to cut ourselves off from emotion in this job. It is a mistake to become too attached to any particular horse. We all have our favourites, our heroes and our villains, but the game is so fickle, balanced on that knife-edge between success and disaster, that feelings should never run any deeper than that.

Sadly, however, attachments, emotions and heartbreak cannot always be avoided, and I reckon every jockey in England felt sorry for Dermot Browne today. Dermot, 'Murphy' as he is known, has always been synonymous with the very good hurdler Brownes Gazette; he has always ridden the horse, and until recently he also owned him. He might have won the Champion Hurdle last March, but poor Dermot was left at the start when the horse spun and jigged sideways when the tapes rose; I, more than anyone, remain thankful for that incident if sympathetic for Dermot's embarrassment. Brownes Gazette was again being aimed for the Champion. Today's Fighting Fifth at Newcastle, in which I had been intended to ride, was the first step along the way. For Brownes Gazette it was also the last step.

I was watching the race on TV in the palatial weighing-room's set under the main stand at Ascot. Along with many other jockeys, I winced and cursed as Brownes Gazette crashed through the rails, for no obvious reason, midway through the race. All too soon, though, it was very evident the horse had suffered a massive heart attack and was dead. I watched poor Dermot, himself unscathed, kneeling by his beloved horse, and thanked God it wasn't me.

My own day, by contrast, was never likely to make headlines

of the right or wrong kind, and when Boom Patrol ran far too freely and faded with utter inevitability up the final hill, I drove home with no great sense of hardship. I was simply glad that tonight my name is not Dermot Browne.

SUNDAY 17 NOVEMBER

The first celebration of the day came with the bleary morning awareness that it was still pouring with rain. Soon, perhaps, some of the best horses available to me, kept so far under protective wraps, will be brought out.

The next good thing was Sunday lunch. A luxury many jockeys, fighting off the excess pounds and forced to resist every temptation, can never contemplate, it is one I seldom like to miss. Today I look Di to the White Hart at Risby, near Bury St Edmunds, a place I can recommend to all. Nancy, who runs the restaurant, recites her menu as if it was the Ten Commandments and I seldom have any trouble polishing off a couple of generous helpings.

MONDAY 18 NOVEMBER

Jump racing is at its worst on Mondays at Leicester. A personal opinion, certainly, but one shared by many in the sport. For one thing, the quality of the programmes is low on Mondays, and for another, Leicester is just about the most dismal, uninspiring course in the country. There is no glamour and laughter here, and I don't know a jockey who enjoys coming. It is, nevertheless, part of the job, and although I woke this morning with a sense of gloom as I reviewed the day ahead and discovered only a single ride in the Leicester seller, the compensations were that the course is only a short drive from home, and that even riding one loser guarantees me a profit of around £25 on the day. It is important to keep such matters in perspective.

I didn't win on the horse but I was back home by three. The ground has certainly eased after the weekend rain but now, as if the fates are conspiring against racing, snow is forecast.

TUESDAY 19 NOVEMBER

With flat racing finished for the year, there are two or three jump meetings almost every day, and it is now that the freelance's job tends to become complicated. The phone calls, both in and out, increase, along with the tricky demands of diplomacy. In my position I can hardly avoid treading on a few toes, disappointing a few people and upsetting a few more; but in all the ducking and diving I must do to sort out my rides, the first priority has always got to be which horses and which meetings are likely to supply me with winners.

It was snowing as I glanced out of the window during my morning session of phoning and book-keeping, but it doesn't look likely to last. It certainly didn't deter me from driving down to London for one of my favourites among the annual racing dos, the Stable Lads Boxing night. Held at the Hilton, it comprises a dinner followed by the boxing and is always great entertainment. As I manage to have my card marked on all the Newmarket lads, there is also a few quid to be made, punting on the fights.

THURSDAY 21 NOVEMBER
Quite a day. My waking hours totalled 20, of which something over eight were spent behind the wheel of my car. It began at 5.00 a.m. with a drive to Lambourn through the murk and mist of an ugly morning. I covered the 134 miles from Newmarket in one hour 50 minutes, schooled six horses for Nicky Henderson, grabbed a swift bite to eat and then climbed back in the car for the long slog north to Haydock Park. I had four rides booked, of which I gave three a decent chance. It was the only no-hoper, Bob Champion's dogged plodder Prince Bai, who provided me with the day's most painful relic, giving me a crashing fall at the final fence, and then adding insult to injury by treading on my nose.

John Jenkins' fancied hurdler Romana ran a bad race; his other runner Shangoseer was not good enough to finish closer than fifth and Kumbi made too many mistakes. Another promising day gone west. I was deflated from lack of a winner and exhausted from the efforts of the day. But there was still one engagement I had no intention of missing. It was the night of the retirement party for John Burke, who has been a close friend and drinking partner for years. I couldn't see him go out of the ranks without being present, so it was back into the car, destination Worcester.

As usual, I forgot my disappointment once I was in sociable company and the time flew. It was 1.00 a.m. by the time I reached my bed for the night in Lambourn, and I felt less tired than I had done eight hours earlier.

FRIDAY 22 NOVEMBER

It goes without saying that Cheltenham gave me my biggest thrills last season, or perhaps of any season. To win the Champion Hurdle on See You Then and the Triumph Hurdle on First Bout in the space of three days gave my career a fantastic lift at an apt time; some said it dragged me from the shadows of J. Francome. I have both horses to ride again this season and, although it could present me with an agonising choice if they both make it to Cheltenham on Champion Hurdle day, I like to think there will be some good days to enjoy on each of them before that. They are two very different horses: See You Then has class and speed, First Bout is a stayer, a streetfighter. But they could both be very good indeed, and today the preparation work began when I schooled First Bout over a few hurdles on the Lambourn gallops. He may have his first run in another three weeks but has some condition to shed before then.

I went on to ride three at Newbury — no luck. My nose is bloody sore and I dread having another fall.

SATURDAY 23 NOVEMBER

If I thought I was in pain last night, it was nothing compared with tonight. I am bruised, battered and, if not quite bowed then admittedly well below par. It is all the fault of a horse called Indamelody who conclusively proved the point that no matter how well a horse may jump during exercise at home it is danger-ous to be confident until he shows it on a racecourse.

It was Hennessy day at Newbury, one of the biggest jumping days of the calendar, and experience had insisted that I set out early and got inside the course fully 90 minutes before the first. I was right, too. The crowds grew to such a pitch that some jockeys and trainers were still absent when we were called to go out for the opening novice hurdle. Josh Gifford and his number one rider Richard Rowe were among the missing men, and it later transpired that they had abandoned their car in the five-mile queue which stretched back from the course onto the M4, and run the remaining distance to the track. All in vain — the first race was run without them.

For some reason I have never quite been able to fathom, the Sloane Ranger population of London appears to descend on Newbury in their entirety every Hennessy day. In their identical Sloane uniforms and with their identical plummy Sloane accents they seem a world apart from most of the regular racegoers and we never see them from one November to the next. But they turn up, they swell the crowd and some of them — the girls, that is — are not at all bad looking, so who am I to complain?

The performance which won the Hennessy deserved a large audience. It was stunning. Galway Blaze was so far superior to this competitive field of chasers that his jockey, Mark Dwyer, was looking around for non-existent dangers as they jumped the cross-fence, five from home. He absolutely trotted up and although he was undoubtedly well-handicapped it gave yet another illustration of just how fine a trainer is Jimmy Fitzgerald. He may train in Malton, an awfully long drive from Newmarket, but I wouldn't mind the chance to get on some of his horses.

My personal calamity followed the big race. It was potentially an exciting novice chase with Indamelody, a good, staying hurdler, The Breener, one of last season's leading novices, and Some Machine, David Nicholson's expensive purchase from Ireland, all jumping fences for the first time. But it became something of a damp squib. Some Machine was tailed off from early on, and my horse never settled at all. He rushed at his fences, attacking them as if they were as small as the hurdles he is used to jumping, and although we survived one bad mistake in front of the stands, he easily got rid of me with another monumental error at the ditch on the far side of the course. At home, he had impressed me with his jumping: it is a different matter in a race.

The fall alone would have been bad enough, but the horse behind ran all over me. I tried to get up but my leg gave way and I sagged back onto the turf. The ambulance men who quickly surrounded me were convinced I had broken my leg and took some elaborate and perhaps over-zealous precautions. I had my legs strapped together and was lifted onto a stretcher for the ambulance ride across the track. The ambulance reversed right up to the door of the medical room, at the back of the weighing-room block, and screens were erected as I was wheeled out. It crossed my mind that some of the gawping sightseers who always gather at such moments might have thought I was dead, when actually the main thing on my mind was convincing the doctor that there was nothing seriously wrong with me at all. I had already investigated the damage in the ambulance and confirmed that the top of my foot was badly swollen. I had also taken a kick on the shin, which was more painful than anything. But I was satisfied that nothing was broken and I managed to brazen it out well enough for the doctor to allow me home rather than recommending a hospital stay. I did have to go for some x-rays, thankfully negative, and when Di got me home I used the ultrasonic lamp we have to treat her horse's injuries in order to disperse the swelling.

SUNDAY 24 NOVEMBER

You find out who your friends are when you have had a bad fall and I was quite touched by the number of phone calls I had today, asking after my progress and wishing me well. The press were on, of course, but a good number of jockeys and other friends called too, and I felt improved enough to astonish them all with the news that I might even ride tomorrow.

MONDAY 25 NOVEMBER

I did not exactly feel up to an early-morning run, but the bruising had begun to go even if much of the aching pain was till there. I found I could just about fit my boot over the injury so I decided to risk it and ride Oversway for Di at Folkestone. I turned down another couple of rides, not wanting to take too many chances, but I was pleased with the way things went. We finished second, running on well, and although I was sore afterwards I'd done it no further damage. I am certainly fit enough to partner my old chum Kathies Lad in a big chase on my local Huntingdon track tomorrow.

Breaking fast out of the 'gate' is crucial to obtaining your position in a race. I stare across at the starter through my distinctive dark goggles, waiting for the moment he brings down his hand to lift the tape. Alan Johnson

On tour with some of my closest jockey mates (LEFT TO RIGHT) Peter Scudamore, Hywel Davies, John Francome and Jonjo O'Neill. 'Franc' and Jonjo are both now training. Caroline Norris

A jockey's valet does very much more than just put out the right silks. John Buckingham even lets me share his ice cream on a hot autumn racing day. Alan Johnson

TOP   *A memorable and emotional winner for me, giving John Francome his first training success with Thats Your Lot at Sandown.*   Alan Johnson

ABOVE   *Nothing went wrong with this leap – Rhythmic Pastimes winning an October hurdle race at Ascot. Later on, his confidence went to pieces.*   Alan Johnson

TOP *Early morning on the Lambourn gallops, My guv'nor Nicky Henderson directs operations.* Fiona Vigors

ABOVE *Away from it all on the French ski-slopes . . . but when will they open that bar?* Courtesy of Steve Smith Eccles

TUESDAY 26 NOVEMBER

Kathies Lad came to the last fence a stride or two behind The Mighty Mac. I was sure we would win. Monica Dickinson's horse is a brilliant jumper and an exciting front-runner, but we had closed steadily on him during the final half-mile and now I had plenty in reserve and felt poised to pounce for the first prize. We met the fence on a long stride, which seemed perfect as Kathies Lad had been jumping really well but now, most unusually, he put down on me — put in an extra short stride — and inevitably got no more than half-way the height of the fence, catapulting me from the saddle and into the ground with a resounding thud. It was exactly what I did not need after the traumas of the past week. Losing out on a good winner was one pain; a third bad fall in a week was another. I managed to get to my feet and hobble to the ambulance this time. Once more, the doctor cleared me to ride tomorrow, but this time I know I have more than bruises to contend with. My head is aching already.

WEDNESDAY 27 NOVEMBER

I was awake at one o'clock this morning, searching for painkillers as the headaches raged. I am probably concussed. The pills allowed me to sleep but I still felt dreadful when daylight came. I should not have ridden at Plumpton, a long and fraught drive from Newmarket . . . but there was the chance of a winner, maybe two, and I am still trailing in the title race. I persuaded myself to go and have regretted the decision ever since.

Of my three rides, two were second and the other fourth. All three might have won, and the last of them, Nicky's I'm Somebody, cruised into a long lead between the last two hurdles and looked uncatchable. The punters who had backed him down to favourite were probably counting their money, and I guess their sums had come to something pretty healthy judging by the angry reception I got as I returned to unsaddle after being caught in the last few strides. They thought I had been caught napping, sitting on my lead instead of riding the horse out. I think they are wrong and that they are talking through their pockets, but I cannot be sure any more. I know I feel rough and that I am now in the middle of a very bad patch, full of falls and defeats.

I am feeling low, my head still thumps and the drive home was desperate. It gave me time, too much time, to think about the past few days and I came to the conclusion that Simon Sherwood will be champion jockey this season. Trainers are jumping on the bandwagon that inevitably surrounds a new and successful name, while some of the trainers I had been counting on are not supporting me as I'd hoped. Simon is riding with tremendous zest and confidence, while right now my own confidence is draining away.

THURSDAY 28 NOVEMBER

At eight this morning I was on the road to London for the Jockey Club appeal, demanded by Freddie Starr after his horse Kings Bridge had been demoted at Devon four weeks ago. I thought we had little chance, but as jockey I had to go. On all known journey times I had left plenty of leeway for the trip to Portman Square and my part of the hearing before scooting back for three rides at Warwick in the afternoon. But a mixture of snow, accidents and traffic jams meant that at 10.20 a.m., ten minutes before the appeal was due to begin, I was stationary, still five miles from the Jockey Club. I took an instant decision, phoned my solicitor at the hearing and told him my plight, then did a U-turn and headed for Warwick.

Immediately, I wondered what on earth I was doing — not only risking the wrath of Mr Starr, but doing so for the dubious privilege of riding Green Bramble and Indamelody, horses who had given me some memorable tumbles. But, if they have sometimes seemed dangerous conveyances, they also both have ability and Green Bramble finally got me off the 29-winner mark which had anchored me for a fortnight, winning gamely with a big weight, while Indamelody got round safely this time.

Drove home with yet another headache and went to bed still not knowing the result of the appeal.

FRIDAY 29 NOVEMBER

I switched on the TV this morning to check whether the Leicester meeting at which I was due to ride had survived a heavy frost, and got a nasty shock. Richard Linley and his wife Beverley were involved in a car crash on icy roads after yesterday's Wincanton meeting. Richard is critically injured and Beverley is dead. And I thought I had problems.

It made me feel sad and sick. I have always maintained that a jump jockey is in as much danger driving in wintry conditions every day as he is out on the track, but that knowledge can never prepare you for death and injury when it happens to friends. It certainly made me reflect that there is more to life than riding horses, and I was not sorry when Leicester was abandoned.

SATURDAY 30 NOVEMBER
Richard remains critical after two major operations. I hear the atmosphere at Sandown yesterday was sombre, and there was still a degree of disbelief among the jockeys there today.

Out of that sorrow, however, emerged a day I shall remember for a long time. I rode one of the most rewarding winners of my career to give J. Francome his first success as a trainer at last. What's more, it was on a horse which went off at 25-1; it was in a big three-year-old hurdle, and it was on TV. So, for John, some good may have come out of that depressing day at Worcester in September. Di was standing with 'Franc' on the huge Sandown terraces and she told me later that he had got surprisingly emotional as the horse, That's Your Lot, skated in by six lengths. He certainly received an incredible ovation in the winner's enclosure.

I went on to finish a close second on Dhofar in the big handicap hurdle, then win the long-distance chase on the remarkable Kumbi, who would be a bloody good horse if ever he learned to jump! My efforts on this one left me ridiculously weak, and I got off my ride in the last and got Di to drive me home. I'm clearly not right. I shouldn't be exhausted like this, even after three testing rides, and I've decided to have a few days off and not ride again until Wednesday.

DECEMBER

MONDAY 2 DECEMBER
Reading is a hobby of mine, a relaxation; nothing too heavy, nothing demanding great intellect or powers of concentration, much more a means of switching off from cares and worries, of escaping from the real world. Wilbur Smith's thrillers, set in South Africa, give me the sort of release I seek from a book. I was just getting stuck into one of his best, my feet up in front of a generous log fire, when John Jenkins phoned. What he had to say persuaded me to revise my immediate plans.

John has asked me to ride Foyle Fisherman for him at Fontwell tomorrow. Nothing remarkable about that until you know that this is one of the horses owned by David Steele, with whom I had understood I was still not exactly flavour of the month. Simon had been riding all his horses recently ... perhaps he has done something to upset him? Anyway, the request was coupled with an offer to ride another of Mr Steele's horses at Cheltenham on Friday. This one, called Ivy League, came over from Ireland with a reputation as high as his price tag. He is reputed to have cost around £120,000, which makes him one of the most expensive National Hunt horses in training. Rides like that one are not to be sniffed at — and if I'm to ride him, I really have to go to Fontwell tomorrow. I can hardly say no.

TUESDAY 3 DECEMBER
Fontwell is a long way for one ride, but it seems a much shorter drive back after a winner. It was a near thing, but I pulled the race out of the bag on Foyle Fisherman, beating Fandango Light a neck after a real battle up the run-in. The horses raced close

together and the jockey of the beaten animal objected, but I was rightly confident the result would stand. Mr Steele was beaming brightly, John Jenkins was happy and I was glad I came back a day early.

It has, in fact, been a long day. I started out around 7.00 a.m., schooling Kathies Lad at Alan Jarvis's place. The plan had been to run the horse in the big 'chase at Cheltenham on Saturday, which would have given me a tricky problem as I have also been asked to ride Duke of Milan in the race. My first really delicate decision of the season has now been made for me, however, as 'Kathies' is clearly not quite right after that heavy fall at Huntingdon last week . . . which makes two of us!

WEDNESDAY 4 DECEMBER

John Francome had some unkind words for the stewards during his career and in one memorably hilarious after-dinner speech he referred to them as 'cabbage patch kids'. Now that he has retired, maybe they are missing his regular visits and want someone to replace him. Me, for instance? Today at Worcester I was called before them twice. They fined me £25 for undoing my chin strap as I walked back after the first race, overruling my plea that the strap was tight and aggravating one of my many recent headaches. Then, later in the afternoon they accepted my explanation for dropping my hands on a desperately tired horse and being touched off for second place — though I had the distinct impression they came within a whisker of 'doing' me for this one, too. The stewards are a necessity on every racecourse and I'm sure most of them do a fine job; but they remain an occupational hazard for every jockey!

It was, all in all, not the happiest of days. My weekend plans are now in chaos as my retaining trainer Nicky Henderson has altered his plans and decided against sending First Bout — last season's Triumph Hurdle winner — to Cheltenham for his seasonal debut. Instead, he is sending me to Lingfield to ride Green Bramble. This means I must pass up four decent outside rides at Cheltenham and involves some reluctant and unpleasant phone calls.

THURSDAY 5 DECEMBER

I went to Uttoxeter for a single ride. Anywhere else and I might have turned it down, but I always combine trips to Uttoxeter with a visit to my parents, who live virtually on the route. We are a close-knit family; my mother, whose philosophy to life is that if you are not eating, you're not very well, loves the chance to feed me up and ruin my weight, and my Dad usually enjoys coming racing with me. Not today, though: he was a good judge.

From the time I left Newmarket this morning to the time I got back tonight, the rain never relented. It was torrential, quite the most spectacular I have seen in ages, and it made for a thoroughly unpleasant day. The racing itself was bad enough — jockeys can wear supposedly waterproof breeches but no garment can protect against that kind of rain. Walking around at the start was miserable for horses and jockeys alike. But the driving was much worse.

I passed three separate accidents on my way to Derbyshire, and the return trip, in equally fierce rain but also in darkness, left my eyes like lumps of lead. I was more exhausted from driving than if I had ridden five or six horses at a meeting, and I could not help thinking of poor Richard Linley. It was this part of our job which was responsible for the death of his wife and for his own serious injuries — the man in the street, even the racing follower who sees jump jockeys at work every week, can never appreciate that often the most exacting part of our business is having to drive long distances each day in the worst weather an English winter can produce.

FRIDAY 6 DECEMBER

David Steele must have thought owning racehorses was an easy route to fame and fortune while Wing and a Prayer and Beat the Retreat were winning race after race last season. He is now beginning to see the other side of the game I have a feeling he is becoming quickly disillusioned. He rang me last night and mentioned quite casually in conversation that Wing and a Prayer was dead — in fact that he died only a couple of days after his last run at Newbury. I was stunned, not so much by the death of the horse but by the fact that John Jenkins had not mentioned it to me either on the phone or at the races. That I found very hard to understand.

Mr Steele had another setback today. So too did I. Ivy League should have won his race at Cheltenham if he was even to begin to justify his lofty reputation and his enormous purchase price, but after running well for a long way he faded to finish eighth. With any other horse you would probably not have been disappointed. With this one, Mr Steele was very plainly dismayed and although I urged him to give the horse another chance, he is already talking about selling him — inevitably at a big loss. Sometimes, I find owners impossible to fathom.

SATURDAY 7 DECEMBER
Luck comes and goes in fickle fashion in this job. You fly for a few weeks, then you spend days on end wondering where on earth the next winner is coming from. You don't have a single fall for an age, then you have five or six in a week.

Simon Sherwood is currently a vivid example of my point. He is still top of the championship but he has not ridden a winner for a fortnight, and today's events at Lingfield just about summed up his current fortunes. First, he somehow forgot to weigh in after finishing third in the three-year-old hurdle. He must, I suppose, have had things on his mind. It was just a careless oversight, but the stewards fined him and disqualified the horse. Then, in the last race of the day, he was aboard the odds-on favourite — a novice hurdler of his brother's called Idleighs Run. He must have thought that this was the race to end his lean run, but instead it made things many times worse. Twice, down at the start, poor Simon was unseated by this very unruly animal. On the second occasion, with the race now certain to start without him, Simon hurled his cap to the ground in a fury while 21 other jockeys hooted with laughter. He later saw the funny side himself, but it took him a time to force a smile.

Ben de Haan is another good rider for whom precious little is going right. Ben now rides the majority of Fred Winter's good horses, the very same horses which made John Francome champion so many times. But now that Ben has landed the job, the stable has hit a bad patch and the winners have dried up. I was pleased to see him put on two fo Sheikh Ali Abu Khamsin's best horses — Half Free and Gaye Brief — at Cheltenham today but it was somehow inevitable both would be beaten.

My day was a mixed one. I had been upset to miss some rides at Cheltenham, and was feeling decidedly sick when, after finishing second on a Nicky Henderson horse behind Franc's That's Your Lot — which I won on a week ago — I heard that one of my lost rides, Copse and Robbers, had won the three-year-old race at headquarters. But things did get better. Di's horse Oversway ran a blinder, just being touched off into second place, and I finished up winning both divisions of the novice hurdle. One of the winners was a horse called Juven Light, trained by Reg Akehurst, and unless this was a freak performance, he could be very high class.

I went home to my first decent dinner in days, the wasting dilemma over again for a while. But, as so often after a few days of strict dieting, I was full up after the starter and simply could not cope with the main course.

SUNDAY 8 DECEMBER
I enjoy schooling, and pride myself on doing it well, but unless the circumstances leave no option I object to trainers asking me to school on a Sunday morning. Eric Eldin left several messages last night asking me to school his one jumper this morning and I'm afraid I ignored them all. What is wrong with the six working days of the week?

MONDAY 9 DECEMBER
Went to a West End theatre this evening for the first time in my life. Growing up in Derbyshire mining country, and then living in Newmarket and being permanently busy, it is something I had just never got around to doing. Tonight, after a lengthy Sports Writer's Lunch in Kensington, Di and I went to see The Sloane Ranger Revue with the Francomes. I hardly knew what to expect and somewhat to my surprise I greatly enjoyed it. In fact I enjoyed the whole day. It all made a change from the usual weekday diet of driving to a racecourse and galloping round.

TUESDAY 10 DECEMBER

Schooled First Bout again at Nicky's place — very pleased. Last week he had been a bit sketchy at the hurdles, the rust of the summer and autumn months showing through, but today he was much more his old self. He goes to Ascot on Saturday but will probably need the race to bring him on to full fitness.

I drove on from Lambourn down to Plumpton in fog. In fact the fog was so bad at the course that I feared they might abandon the meeting. I only had one ride, Foyle Fisherman again in the second race on the card, so as soon as the first-race jockeys had filed out of the weighing-room I galloped through and weighed out. That little trick ensured I would be paid my riding fee even if they abandoned after one race. I don't think David Steele would have been too pleased if that had happened but in the event the meeting went on, visibility improved, and Foyle Fisherman cheered him up by winning easily.

WEDNESDAY 11 DECEMBER

When I started my career with Tom Jones, there were plenty of jumping trainers in and around Newmarket. They all tended to run their horses at Huntingdon whenever possible, and as I was the locally-based rider I usually had a full book of rides there. For some years now I have been top jockey on the course but with Newmarket now housing so few jump trainers my supply of mounts from the area has dwindled quite alarmingly. I only had two rides there today, neither of which finished in the frame. It remains my favourite track and I know my way round it better than anyone else riding, but I would welcome a few more opportunities to prove it.

THURSDAY 12 DECEMBER

We had quite a house-party last night, the guests including John Francome, Simon Sherwood and Di's brother Tim Thomson-Jones. So out on the gallops this morning Mrs Di Haine, small-time permit trainer, had a celebrated team of riding-out Jockeys. Tim, however, was not at his best. The after-effects of the dinner party were all too plain when he schooled a horse called Tar Flame over hurdles. He clattered clumsily through two flights before Tim pulled him up and demanded to know if we had had the damned horse's eyes tested. When I got on him myself I could see his point. Although I managed to pop him over a couple of fences he was jumping very stiffly. When a horse can't or won't bend his back there is usually something wrong in that area, and we will have to get him checked.

Simon left us to drive down to Somerset and visit Richard Linley in hospital. There just hasn't been time for me to get down there yet, but I have sent Richard a crate of half-bottles of champagne. He may not consider he has much worth celebrating right now, but anything which cheers him up a little must be worth trying.

FRIDAY 13 DECEMBER
And I'm glad I am not superstitious about such things! Racing was at Warwick today, and I positioned myself by the door of the weighing-room as the lads went out to ride in the novice chase. As they filed past I shouted: 'It's Friday the 13th boys — just hang in there!'

It was not the luckiest of days for some. Tim was kicked in the face, fracturing a cheekbone, and Kevin Mooney was stood down for seven days with concussion. Me? I just got beaten on two favourites.

SATURDAY 14 DECEMBER
In our hearts I honestly think both Nicky Henderson and I were convinced that First Bout would be beaten today. He is not fully wound up, he had not raced since March, and was in a pretty hot contest at Ascot. Both of us would have been pleased if he had finished in the first three. But perhaps he is even better than either of us think, because he slaughtered his opposition and won virtually as he pleased. I knew from some way out that I could pick off the others and, jumping superbly, he strode away up the straight to win very impressively.

The bookmaker reaction was predictable but premature. They now make him joint-favourite for next March's Champion Hurdle with See You Then, our other star and current holder of the hurdling crown. I think they are wrong. First Bout is a very nice

74

horse and, personally, I can't wait to ride him over fences when the time comes. But in terms of a Champion Hurdle, I don't think he is in the same class as See You Then. If I had to make my decision now which one to ride in the big race, it would not take me long to make up my mind.

Today's other big meeting was at Doncaster and, between races at Ascot, I watched events up there on the weighing-room television. Hywel Davies had a shocking fall in the two-mile chase, and I recalled that it was at Doncaster last season that he might have been lucky to come out alive from an even more horrific tumble. I wondered what he thought when he went back to the course. It is certainly true that most jockeys have bogy courses, where nothing ever goes right for them and where, eventually, they dread having to ride.

MONDAY 16 DECEMBER
Richard Linley is, naturally enough, still a daily topic of conversation among the jockeys. The bulletins we are receiving now are more encouraging. His condition seems to be improving steadily. But any mention of his plight inevitably creates a sombre mood so it was good to be able to laugh today over something which happened to him. Beverley's parents are apparently keen wine-makers, and they took a bottle into Richard when they visited him a few days ago. At 2.00 a.m. that night there was a dramatic explosion next to Richard's bed which set nurses running in all directions, panicking because they thought a bomb had gone off. It turned out that the home-made wine had popped its cork rather extravagantly. The bottle had smashed, the cork had made a hole in the hospital ceiling, and Richard was discovered in fits of laughter.

This was related to me at Leicester where I rode one winner (Indamelody getting his jumping together) and felt certain I had ridden two. It was a desperately close thing between my horse Paulatim and Cross Master but, looking across on the line as I always do, I judged that I had won by a head. Cross Master's jockey plainly thought so, too, as he steered his horse straight into the runners-up position in the unsaddling enclosure. I duly swung into the winner's spot, exchanged a few cheerful words with

75

Nicky, and had returned to weigh-in when the announcement came that I had been beaten by a head. I could hardly believe the evidence of the photograph.

It was a mad evening — predictably mad, as I had been driven to the races by Jeff Barlow. It is only a 75-mile run from Leicester to Newmarket and we were both finished riding by three o'clock, but it was after 11.00 p.m. when I staggered into my house, led astray again and dallying dangerously in our favourite watering-hole, The Haycock on the A1.

TUESDAY 17 DECEMBER

Foyle Fisherman was sent to Folkestone today aiming for his third victory on consecutive Tuesdays. He failed gallantly, finishing third in a race which would have done justice to a far grander meeting than this one, but despite the fact that penalties had increased his load to 12-2 and he was conceding pounds to the two horses which beat him, David Steele was inconsolable. He now wants to sell this one as well as Ivy League. I think he is wrong, as both horses are sure to win more races, but the owner pays the bills and what he says is law.

From Folkestone I followed the fast motorway route back to Lambourn, taking the M20, M26, M25 and M4, thankful as I drove that I am having my career in an age when long journeys can be undertaken without much recourse to slow country roads or even slower, unreliable trains.

At Nicky Henderson's Windsor House yard we had an early-evening conference, also involving head lad 'Corky' Brown. We talked through the horses one by one, mapping out plans and hopes for each of them. It was a productive discussion. Nicky has a high-class team of horses here this season and he is sensibly being patient with the big guns. We still, for instance, don't accurately know when See You Then will reappear on the race-course, but there will be no hurry with him. The Champion, in March, is really the only race which matters.

WEDNESDAY 18 DECEMBER

No jockey is perfect. Even John Francome was not infallible — he made the occasional blunder; but what made him the best was that his cock-ups were far less frequent than anyone else's. There are times when you make a mistake so bad and so obvious that the best policy is to admit it and apologise. That happened to me today. I had gone to Worcester for one ride — Jeff King's Veleso in a three-mile handicap chase. I won three times on the horse last season, and although he was not expected to add to that score today he might well have run decently. But he didn't get the chance. I fell off him at the first fence. He didn't make much of a mistake, just put in an extra short stride: but I fell off. As there were plenty of runners, and I was upsides in front when we met the fence, I took the inevitable kicking as the rest of the field galloped over me. I was not badly hurt, but the ambulance picked me up anyway, and on the way back across the course I agonised over what I should say to Jeff. Having been a brilliant jockey himself, Jeff tends to judge everyone else by his own standards and so is a notoriously hard taskmaster. I knew that if I trumped up an excuse he would crucify me, so I didn't even try. As he walked to meet me I just said: 'Sorry Jeff, I fell off.' I waited for the explosion but, instead, he burst out laughing. Honesty really is often the best policy.

THURSDAY 19 DECEMBER
My life has just flashed before me. I feel so shaken I cannot think straight. I have come within an inch of killing someone. I have also done untold damage to my car, let alone my nerves. I was almost home when it happened. The annual Bollinger dinner took place in London last night and I stayed down, heading back up the M10 this morning as I had no rides booked anywhere. I had left the motorway and was travelling at moderate speed along a country road when, up ahead of me, an accident unfolded. It was a strange experience. I knew it was going to happen and I was powerless to do anything about it. A car was backing out of a drive. A motorbike was approaching at high speed. As if in slow motion, I saw the inevitable collision, winced at a noise like a gunshot and watched in horror as the rider of the motorbike cartwheeled high into the air and flew towards me. He hit the road with a sickening thud and slid into my path. I was not moving that fast but it still required rapid reactions to swing the car off

the road — the only place I could go to avoid him. I skidded across the verge and came to rest in a hedge. When I extricated myself the bike-rider was already getting some attention. He was in a bad way but he was alive. He was also lying right next to my tyre-mark. When I got home I was literally shaking, both at what had happened and what might have happened. And after all the bad conditions I have driven in recently, this occurred in bright daylight on a dry, mild morning.

FRIDAY 20 DECEMBER
Loyalty rates high in my book, so when the Lambourn trainer David Murray-Smith rang up today to offer me the ride on Rhyme'n'Reason, second favourite for tomorrow's Welsh Grand National, I had to turn it down. I have already taken the ride on Ginger McCain's enigmatic Kumbi, and although form dictates that he has far less chance than Rhyme'n'Reason I shall not desert him or let down Ginger. I can't pretend I didn't feel a few pangs of regret at refusing, however, and I was not in the best of moods as I drove up into Norfolk for this afternoon's meeting at Fakenham.

The day was bitterly cold and miserably damp, which made Fakenham the last place on earth a jockey would want to be. Condensation dripped on my head from the weighing-room ceiling as I sipped a cup of tea and surveyed the surroundings. There was one wash-basin, one urinal and one shower between 30-odd jockeys. There was no hot water at all. This was the downbeat end of the racing scale, one that those who only frequent Ascot and Cheltenham will never know.

It did, however, have its compensation in the shape of a winner. Gavin's Boom Patrol came here today and I regarded him as a bonking certainty. He was backed down to even-money and he did the job, but made hard work of it, only winning by half a length. I'm afraid he is not the horse we thought he was. At least it meant Gavin's lads had something to celebrate, and some cash in their pockets, at their Christmas party tonight. I went along through a sense of duty. I don't enjoy large gatherings of stable-lads because they not only have very good memories but generally jaundiced memories too. They will mercilessly remind you of each and every occasion you got beaten on a horse they had backed, but they seem to forget the winners!

SATURDAY 21 DECEMBER

The last day of racing before the brief Christmas recess was a mixed and surprising one. I got a lift down to Chepstow with Bob Champion (though I get so screwed up inside, sitting in a passenger seat, I am much better off driving myself) and as we discussed the meeting ahead I thought that I was likely to win the juvenile hurdle on Ana Waslawi but that I was unlikely to win on either of my other booked rides. I was completely wrong.

Ana Waslawi, who cost £20,000-plus, had run very well to be second behind That's Your Lot a fortnight ago and although he often misbehaves at home we had high hopes that he would develop into something pretty useful. But today I am afraid his temperament let him down disastrously, and as the field turned into the back straight I was already in trouble. The horse was digging in his toes and trying to pull up, plainly determined to take no serious part in the race. I got him round, but he trailed in at the back of the field and I could only suggest to Nicky and the owners that they rapidly have him gelded before trying again. If that fails he could turn out to be a quick and very expensive flop.

It was a very different story on Nicky's Pikes Peak in the two-and-a-half-mile novice hurdle. He won in the style of a very good horse, and I will look forward to riding him again. And then there was Kumbi, running the race of his life to finish third in the Welsh National. Rhyme'n'Reason, eventually ridden by Frank Berry, was a long way behind me, so on this occasion loyalty paid off.

Mark Perrett's desperate bad luck goes on. Only just recovered from a broken leg, and still short of rides since his split with Stan Mellor, he got on a good horse of Jenny Pitman's called Smiths Man in the National — and broke his leg again. He didn't even fall, simply felt the leg snap. Not surprisingly he came back in agony and I should think his season is over. Only a year ago people were talking of him as a future star, a potential champion ... it can be a very cruel game, this.

Before leaving the course I handed out my first Christmas gift, a bottle of scotch to the valets. John Buckingham, famous for winning the Grand National on the 100-1 shot Foinavon, is my personal valet, but all of them do a tremendous job under some-times very trying conditions. Their day starts hours before the first jockey arrives at a course and ends considerably after the last one has left. They seldom see a race run, they have to put up with a lot of moaning — not to mention a lot of mud — but they manage to stay quite amazingly cheerful.

MONDAY AND TUESDAY 23 AND 24 DECEMBER
The days when most people buy their final presents: the days when I buy all of mine.

I've told all my trainers that I will not ride at lighter than 10 stone 7 pounds over the next week, which gives me some leeway to indulge my appetite. My parents are due to come and stay with Di and I, but it hardly seems like Christmas yet. It has been a busy time recently and even now, late on Christmas Eve, I am still arranging my holiday rides.

WEDNESDAY 25 DECEMBER
Unlike machines, racehorses cannot be switched off when the workforce is on holiday. So at 7.30 a.m. on this Christmas morn-ing I was out on the Newmarket gallops, giving Di's chaser Oversway a piece of work. He is due to run at Newbury next Monday, and even Christmas Day cannot disrupt a horse's race preparation. From breakfast-time onwards, however, I did not give horses, trainers or racecourses another thought. I ate and drank too much. I enjoyed it, too.

THURSDAY 26 DECEMBER
Kempton Park on Boxing Day is one of the big jump-race meet-ings of the season. It is also one of the most hectic, and crowds clog up the M3 and all other approach roads to Sunbury hours before the scheduled start. Like the Sloane Rangers at Newbury on Hennessy day, there is a peculiar breed of spectator attracted to this meeting. The racing is so good that thousands of regular racefans are always present, but the once-a-year brigade are there in their droves, curing their hangovers and their excesses in the

open air or dragging along unwilling children to avoid another day of mending broken toys. Kempton does not have limitless viewing facilities, and on Boxing Days there are always hundreds perched in positions from which they can see no more than the flash of colours as the horses gallop past. Some experience it once and never come again. Others are hooked by the atmosphere of Bank Holiday escapism, of Christmas cigars and new coats, and come back each year. All I can add is that anyone who left Kempton with a smile today was lucky. Rain was falling steadily when I got up this morning and it set the tone for one of the most miserable Boxing Days I can recall. I left Newmarket very early to beat the crowds, and got to Kempton in time to enjoy a game of pool. But once the racing began any glamour apparently attached to this prestigious day was stripped away. All that was left was a freezing wind, driving rain and flying mud. Goggles were useless after a few hundred yards; there was nothing for it but to pull them down and take the mud full in the face. The thought of a blazing log fire, a lunchtime drink and a decent Boxing Day meal flashed mischievously across my mind and I wondered what on earth I was doing in this job. The feeling always passes, usually hastened by a winner, but today even that tonic was missing.

First Bout ran a stinking race. After his impressive win at Ascot it was too bad to be true. I was struggling a mile out, and although he plugged on to finish fourth he felt anything but a champion. This Christmas Hurdle has become a bogy race for Nicky Henderson; last year See You Then ran equally badly in the race. But he went on to triumph at Cheltenham. So why should Nicky worry about the omens now?

Wayward Lad won the King George again, at long odds. The pundits had written him off as a light of other days, and considered that the race was between Combs Ditch and Burrough Hill Lad. But for some reason Wayward Lad often sparkles at Kempton. Graham Bradley gave him a lovely ride and I was delighted for him — he is one of the best northern jockeys, if not the best.

FRIDAY 27 DECEMBER
Back to Kempton with a heavy heart for the second day of the

holiday meeting, perennially as different from the first as lemon-ade is from champagne. After the heady excitement and the huge crowds of Boxing Day, normality reluctantly returns. There is an ordinary crowd for an ordinary card, but at least the sun shone.

I had only two rides, both for Nicky Henderson, and neither of them won. I'm having another quiet spell now, but I was sharply reminded of how rapidly fortunes can change when Richard Dun-woody rode four consecutive winners, after almost three weeks without a winner at all.

I cheered myself up in the time-honoured way, by eating. Another of Kempton's popular features among the jockeys is the tearoom, where a lady called Josie fusses around us like a mother hen and provides some super sandwiches. In fact, if it wasn't for the racing, I might have enjoyed the last two days much more!

SATURDAY 28 DECEMBER
The ground was white with frost when I peered out of the bedroom window this morning. My first thought was that there would be no racing today, and my second thought was that that would suit me fine. True, it was Newbury I would be missing, a good meeting on a favourite course, but when your luck is out and your energy low even those like myself, lucky enough to enjoy their job, begin to run short of enthusiasm. The radio confirmed my impression. There would be no racing anywhere in the country. I settled contentedly for a weekend at home and dug out a Jack Higgins thriller to see me through to the start of 'Grandstand'.

MONDAY 30 DECEMBER
As we are still frozen solid and Newbury is off again, I booked an appointment to have my hair cut this afternoon. But I never got there. Just after breakfast Alan Jarvis phoned to ask if I was free to go and work some of his horses on the beach at Yarmouth. I agreed to go along and I'm glad I did. Galloping along at the water's edge with the wind blowing in fresh off the sea gave me a feeling that was both solitary and exhilirating. It was another side of racing, an unexpected side. I didn't get my haircut but I had a good day.

TUESDAY 31 DECEMBER

This is the half-way point in the season, and a bleak one at that. There was no racing in England for the third day running, and I'm no longer happy about it. I've had my break, now I am eager to get back riding, chasing the winners, striving to be champion. I'm in there fighting, still in second place behind Simon Sherwood and very much within striking distance. I have got through so far without serious injury. There have been plenty of falls, plenty of highs and lows. But the really big days of the season are still to come. The reckoning is still in front of us all.

JANUARY

WEDNESDAY 1 JANUARY

Bank Holidays mean nothing to jockeys. Nothing, that is, except a confusion of meetings from which to choose, and the regular suspicion that you are in a national minority in not having a hangover when the day begins. I was sensible last night — a few drinks with some friends and to bed not long after the New Year struck — and my compensations this morning were a clear head and a clear road for the drive to Cheltenham, where the major holiday meeting was staged. It was not, however, a good road. After a cold night ice lay in lethal patches on the surface, and I passed four separate accidents on the short stretch of motorway between Newmarket and Huntingdon. Although I was at the wheel of Di's mother's Mercedes, my car being in dock after the pre-Christmas prang, I kept to a steady speed. One idiot flashed past, doing something over 100 mph. I glanced across and confirmed that, in the usual style of motoring maniacs, he had a beard!

The two best novice hurdlers seen out this season won at Cheltenham. Ten Plus, trained by Fulke Walwyn, was the first to go in and I won the other division on Nicky's Pikes Peak. It will be some race, if and when these two meet back at Cheltenham in March, but an awful lot can happen before then.

THURSDAY 2 JANUARY

Racing's betting underworld has been alive with fanciful rumours that all is not well with See You Then. Based presumably on the fact that he has not appeared in public since winning his crown last March, the gossip has it that he will not be ready to defend his title, and some of the bookies have taken sufficient notice to extend his odds. I can tell you, however, that if jockeys were allowed to bet I would plunge heavily on him now. Nothing, to my mind, will get near him on the big day.

I say this despite suffering an unnerving indignity when I schooled the horse today for the first time this season. No sooner had my backside touched the saddle than I was unceremoniously bucked off. As I flew gracelessly through the air I caught a fleeting glimpse of Nicky Henderson's face. It was a portrait of shock and alarm and I could well imagine what was flashing through his mind. Day one of the champion's proper preparation, and here he was about to set off around the Berkshire countryside, capable of causing untold damage, chiefly to himself. To Nicky's eternal relief, not to mention mine, I had managed to cling onto the reins and made certain that the damage was confined to a couple of bruises on my own body and pride. See You Then, having had his fun, was far more amenable to being mounted second time around, and proceeded to jump like a stag. We could not be more pleased with the way he has come on. Physically he has developed very well and, while there will still be no rush to get him onto a racecourse, I cannot see a hurdler to beat him right now.

First Bout certainly shouldn't beat him. He ran again at Cheltenham today in a two-and-a-half-mile race. Ran well, too, finishing third behind two older horses in Corporal Clinger and Galas Image. Kempton can now at least be dismissed as a freakishly bad day — but I still have no doubts which of our two horses I want to be on in March.

A surprise and welcome face at Cheltenham today was Sam Morshead. All of us in the weighing-room have been concerned about Sam as he has been absent since a fall on the flat at Warwick all of five weeks ago. His concussion was so serious that he apparently could not walk downstairs without feeling dizzy. He is still not fully recovered now and, although it was good to see him back amongst us I wonder if he will see this as a sign that his career might not have long to go.

FRIDAY 3 JANUARY

Fred Winter phoned up to offer me a ride at Sandown tomorrow. This is only because he runs two horses in the race and one of his retained riders, Jimmy Duggan, is being sent to the other meeting at Warwick, but it still gave me a kick. When Fred asks you to ride for him you can't be too bad a pilot.

SATURDAY 4 JANUARY
Fred Winter phoned again. Warwick is off, Duggan is available so yours truly is not needed after all. Still, the thought was there. Sandown, all things considered, was a bit of a disaster as Indamelody, who seemed to have taken to jumping fences after his temperamental start, put me over his head again. Horse and rider unhurt — but it's back to the drawing-board with this one.

Pete Scudamore won yet another big race, this time the Anthony Mildmay-Peter Cazalet Chase, on Run And Skip. He is riding like a demon, and was absolutely brilliant today.

MONDAY 6 JANUARY
After winning my regular Sunday night snooker match 6-0 I went out this morning and invested in my own cue. I just might start to take this game seriously — the way things are going I could end up making more money from snooker than from racing. The weather has closed in again. Nottingham was frosted off today, and there is not much hope for tomorrow.

WEDNESDAY 8 JANUARY
As it's a few degrees warmer down south I got up this morning full of hope that I would be heading for Plumpton to ride a decent novice of Jeff King's. Switched on the radio and what do I hear? Plumpton is waterlogged! That's the trouble with this time of year — the weather operates in extremes, and if racing is not off for one thing it will be off for another. It plays hell with us poor jockeys trying to plan our lives.

THURSDAY 9 JANUARY
Back to work. Wincanton is often a good bet for a resumption after a spell of abandonments; it's a popular track, both with the working fraternity of trainers and jockeys and with the paying public. There is a hard core of West Country farmers who come to every meeting, and I happen to know that the course attracts fans from consider-

able distances. It's not that it is very accessible, either. Quite the opposite in fact. You approach the course down some winding, hedge-bordered country lanes which begin to look as if they lead nowhere; it is not near a single large town and is, in fact, one of the least convenient of all the southern tracks to reach.

For all that, it was good to see the lads for the first time since Saturday, and good to be earning again. Most people tend to forget that a jockey's income abruptly dries up when the weather halts racing. Only those with seasonal retainers have anything to fall back on. I had only the one ride but I expected him to win. It was Ogden York, a novice hurdler which Di used to train. He's now with John Francome, and he had twice run well without winning, so we had every right to fancy him today. But he was a big disappointment, disliking the soft ground and dropping into the also-rans very quickly. 'Franc', however, is not one of those trainers who will mope and moan about such setbacks. Five minutes after the race he was in the weighing-room for a cup of tea, laughing and joking with us just the same as he used to be when riding. I must say I admire this phlegmatic side of his nature, even if it has tended to offend the more serious-minded people in our sport. John's attitude to life is that there is always a tomorrow, so why worry. It's an outlook which should ensure he lives a long time.

FRIDAY 10 JANUARY

Schooling half-a-dozen horses in pouring rain soon after dawn is not always my idea of a good time, but it served its purpose today. All six of them jumped well and I was able to sweat off an excess pound or two. I've been as fat as a pig since Christmas, and the shortage of recent racing has not helped one bit. I managed to do 10 stone 3 pounds on Green Bramble today at Ascot, but the horse is still not right. He ran left-handed at every fence, losing about three lengths each time, and in the circumstances he did well to finish fourth in a race marred by Brown Chamberlin breaking down. He has always been a bad-legged horse, but plenty of people had begun to fancy him quietly for the Gold Cup. Simon Sherwood had been paid a big retainer to ride him for the rest of the season. This was only the second time he had sat on him, and it will also be the last. Barring a miracle, Brown Chamberlin will never run again.

SATURDAY 11 JANUARY

My quiet time goes on, but 'Scu' can do no wrong. He rode a double at Ascot today, and has now overtaken me and gone into second place in the table. His greatest quality is his strength in a finish, and that was evident on both today's winners, Tickete Boo and Very Promising. I can say with absolute certainty that a weaker, less experienced jockey would have been beaten on them both and I was staggered to hear that there had been some phone calls to the course from TV viewers complaining the 'Scu' had overused his whip. That may have been a valid criticism of his riding in his early days, but not any more. If those armchair critics had been a shade more observant they would have seen that although 'Scu' uses his stick very vigorously he is for much of the time either waving it past the horse's head or slapping him harmlessly down the shoulder.

As for me, I seem to be following my annual pattern. Don't ask me why, but I always suffer a famine of winners during January. I might just as well pack up for two or three weeks and grab that much-needed holiday.

MONDAY 13 JANUARY

If Sunday racing ever does come to Britain, and I have very mixed feelings about the prospect, it might have one welcome side-benefit. Mondays could then be scrapped as a racing day — you would not hear a single moan from the jockeys' room. The cards on a Monday are invariably uninspiring, and the venues are no better. I usually end up going to one of the dreary midland courses to race in front of a few hundred diehards. Leicester runs it close but for me, Wolverhampton is the most soulless course of the lot; with my confidence short and my luck poor, I drove there today in hardly the sunniest of spirits. It gave me my first winner since 1 January!

It was a typical Wolverhampton day — cold, grey and with the threat of rain. It was a typical Wolverhampton card, too, and although I had three reasonable rides I have reached the stage where I didn't expect any of them to win. When Bright Arrow, one of Nicky's young hurdlers, stopped suddenly in the straight from a promising position I thought it was an omen for another blank day, but my old pal J. Francome came to the rescue, and I rode his useful flat horse Asswan to win the other division of the novice hurdle.

WEDNESDAY 15 JANAURY

Are retainers worthwhile? I found myself asking that question again today as my commitment to Nicky caused more headaches for the weekend ahead. Already, I have had to turn down a couple of potential winners to ride inferior horses for the Henderson yard. It's not Nicky's fault; he offered me the retainer, I took it, and naturally I'm pleased enough to have the link when his top horses run. But there is no doubt at all that a retainer complicates life. It means that I am not a genuine freelance any more, and I am not convinced that I like the restriction. This is something to consider for next season, I think.

I got a shock when I stepped on the scales at Windsor today. I was 10 stone 5 pounds stripped, which meant I could not possibly ride at less than 10 stone 8 pounds. I have never been so heavy and I can't quite understand it. It cost me a ride today, as Jeff King was understandably adamant that he would not put up five pounds overweight on a handicap chaser, and although the horse concerned trailed in last under Simon Sherwood, I am going to have to do something about the problem before it takes root.

Windsor is one of England's two figure of eight tracks, Fontwell being the other, and they certainly take some riding. If you get a horse on the inside rail for one bend, he will be on the outside for the next bend, so a good deal of dodging about is called for; small wonder that some horses don't act very happily on this track.

'Scu' rode another winner. I didn't, and drove home with only a supper-less night to look forward to.

THURSDAY 16 JANUARY

No breakfast, no lunch, and yet again no winners. It was desperate ground at Lingfield (it's always bottomless mud there even if the ground is good elsewhere), but the day did have its redeeming features. I am still fit and healthy, which is saying something, the rate jockeys are getting hurt at present. And I finished up spending a sociable evening in London with my pal and rival, S. Sherwood. At times of adversity, enjoy yourself — that's my motto.

FRIDAY 17 JANUARY

The racing hacks were out in force at Kempton this evening. Nicky had arranged for See You Then to have a racecourse gallop with two of his other horses, and it seems that to many people this was the big event of the day. A lot of the crowd stayed on and they cannot have been disappointed at what they saw. The rumour-mongers who had been renaming the horse See You When must have slunk away silently as he cruised past the two stablemates, jumping brilliantly. He blew hard afterwards, as you would expect, but I told anyone who asked that I consider him a ten-pound better horse than he was last season, and I am more convinced than ever that he will win at Cheltenham.

I am also becoming increasingly convinced that 'Scu' will be champion jockey. Maybe it's a maudlin view from the depths of my bad patch, but I honestly think he will take some catching, the way he is riding right now. When you are in a purple patch like this, you ride with enormous confidence, and Peter won a race today that summed it up perfectly. Solar Cloud, the four-year-old he was riding, veered all over the course, yet 'Scu' kept him going to win by a neck. If he had been out of form and low on confidence, he would have been beaten.

SATURDAY 18 JANUARY

The big races were at Doncaster and Kempton, but I went to the bread-and-butter meeting at Warwick, with no complaints, though. I rode a welcome winner, Paulatim, winning the novice chase in comfortable style. Nicky's main object in sending me here, I think, was to ride an ex-Irish hurdler called Charlie's Cottage. They have expected a lot of this horse and Nicky had plainly not lost faith despite several disappointments. But today, tried over a new, longer trip, he not only never looked like winning, he also made a very unhealthy noise. There may well be something substantially wrong with him. He is certainly not the horse they thought he was when they bought him.

MONDAY 20 JANAURY

Di knows now not to bother cooking me any dinner when I go racing with the Newmarket Musketeers. It was the usual routine today. Short drive to Leicester, one ride on a no-hoper, finished work by 3.00 p.m., home by 11.00 p.m. ...

TUESDAY 21 JANUARY

I knew as soon as I took the ride that I had made a mistake. It was only the fact that it was John Burke who phoned me which lowered my guard. Burkey is such a good old mate that I'd love to help him out in his new career as an assistant trainer. He offered me two rides at Nottingham today, one in a novice hurdle, the other in the novice chase. Neither had any chance, but I took them anyway.

On the way up the A1 this morning I had second thoughts. There was a maximum field for the novice chase. I had nothing to prove; it was too risky. I asked John when I got there to find someone else, and immediately felt relieved. It was funny how things turned out. It was not the novice chase but the hurdle which caused the carnage ... I was out the back, just concentrating on getting round safely and teaching the horse a little. One fell in front of me, bringing down two more. Suddenly, there was nowhere to go, and as I crossed the hurdle I knew we were galloping all over one of the prostrate jockeys. I had no clear idea who it was but I heard the crunch as we hit him, felt the shock waves shoot up my horse's legs and knew instantly that I had done the bloke some serious damage. As soon as I had weighed in after the race I headed for the ambulance room, and there he was. It turned out to be a young claimer called David Chinn and he looked as if he had been trampled on by a herd of hungry elephants. His silks were ripped to shreds and the doctor was busily engaged in literally stitching his ear back on. Meanwhile, a couple of other jockeys were also being treated and Anthony Webber was being dispatched to hospital. It was a depressing mess, even though there was nothing at all I could have done about it.

WEDNESDAY 22 JANUARY

The Musketeers led me astray again last night, The Haycock Inn taking our custom until a late hour. Unusually for me I had a thick head this morning, and didn't exactly relish the long drive to dismal Wolverhampton. It was raining and blowing a gale, but it was still worth going. Smart Reply, the American-bred horse of Nicky's which had disappointed over hurdles, took to fences much more readily and won by 30 lengths. That was my 44th winner of the season, and although I have had a long lean run, I am actually closing the gap on Simon — now only five behind.

It occurred to me on the unpleasant drive home that this time last year I was lying on a beach in Barbados.

THURSDAY 23 JANUARY
The best thing about today's racing was that I didn't have far to come home! It was at Huntingdon, but even my favourite course failed to cheer me or change my current luck. I not only drew a blank, which is becoming a familiar January tale, but I also inwardly accepted that I am really not riding with my usual zest and confidence. It is a worrying admission, but an honestly-held view. I am finding it very hard to rouse myself for the run-of-the-mill race days which, after all, dominate the jockey's calendar. Apart from longing for a holiday, I am also anxious for the major occasions to hurry along, those days when I need no motivating to test myself and my mounts against the best.

I could have fancied each of my three rides today, but a second on Nicky Henderson's four-year-old, Attiki, was the closest I came to scoring. Di's Oversway just failed to stay three miles, and John Francome's Ogden York ran as if he is in the same state as me — a bit run-down and in need of a rest!

FRIDAY 24 JANUARY
Doncaster is one of those crossover northern courses, like Haydock Park, and to a lesser extent Wetherby, at which southern jockeys will appear now and again to ride in major races. These three tracks would be the north's equivalent of Sandown, Ascot and Kempton, where we often see the leading northern riders down for big events. Today's card on the Town Moor course at Doncaster was not all that special apart from a valuable novice hurdle, called the Rossington Main, which is annually competitive, and this year had drawn a better field than ever. There were about a dozen previous winners lining up, including the horse I had driven up there to ride, Asswan. I knew

there were a number of fancied runners, and I honestly had no idea how well my horse would fare against them but as it turned out he beat them all ... then lost the race to an unconsidered 50-to-1 shot.

As usual at Doncaster the ground was good and fast, which greatly appealed to my horse — and, as usual, the wind whipped mercilessly across the moor, cutting through the silks and chilling all of us jockeys to the bone. I was pleased, though, to be riding only in the big hurdle event. I have long held a dread of the Doncaster fences, which I believe to be the worst in the country. They are so formidably big and bushy that they deter horses, even some usually good jumpers, and there always appear to be too many falls here for comfort.

I had driven Jeff Barlow to the meeting. He had ridden two hurdlers at Huntingdon yesterday, both of which had fallen, and when he fell again in the opening hurdle race today I have a feeling his confidence for his ride in the later novice chase was at a pretty low ebb. I wished him well, silently glad that I was staying in the weighing-room, and I was as relieved as he was to see him return safely after an uneventful ride round.

SATURDAY 25 JANUARY

My situation in Newmarket has plenty of advantages, but I have to say that on mornings like this one it is not the most convenient place to live. Frost had bitten into the ground nationwide overnight, and inspections were called at all four planned meetings. Three of them — Ayr, Doncaster and Folkestone, were rapidly abandoned, but at Cheltenham, the feature card of the day and the place where I had five booked rides, a decision was delayed several times. I could understand the course management's anxiety to keep the meeting on; in other circumstances, I would openly have applauded their efforts. But as I hovered restlessly at home between the telephone and the radio I admit to wishing they had called it off at eight o'clock and had done with it.

Eventually I set off, grimly daring them to call it off when I was half-way through the long, westward journey. But they didn't, and although when I got to Prestbury Park I discovered that my five rides had been whittled down to three — one withdrawn due to the ground and another reclaimed by a re-routed Peter Scudamore — it was still a good card on which I had two genuine winning chances.

I might easily have won on them both. Prime Oats, one of Nicky's best four-year-olds and having only his second run over hurdles, ran very well indeed in the Triumph Hurdle Trial and in my view would have won but for being hampered by the eventual third just before jumping the last. Even after that he was only narrowly beaten by Tangognat, who is currently favourite for the Triumph in March. I'm not afraid of him.

At this time of year the Triumph is still a lottery. I would never have an ante-post bet in it even if I was allowed to — much of the early form is unreliable and first-year jumpers tend to run in and out of form before settling down as they gain experience. Prime Oats has not even won a race yet and if he should go to Cheltenham still a maiden he has a chance of being ballotted out of an always over-subscribed event. But if he takes his place in the line-up, then on what I know and have seen of the juveniles this season, I shall look forward to a very good ride on him.

By contrast, I don't know if I shall ever sit on Misty Spirit again, but I was certainly grateful to pick up the ride on him today. He is trained in the north by a man named Don Lee, and I confess I had never heard of him until he phoned to book me. I thought at first the horse would have no chance as the opposition included the long-range Gold Cup favourite Dawn Run, over from Ireland to gain experience of the Cheltenham fences. But when I took a closer look at the race I realised I was not entirely without hope. My horse had a decent, consistent record in northern handicaps, whereas Dawn Run, for all her brilliant ability, is still not the steadiest of jumpers; I had severe reservations about her prospects of putting in a clear round at Cheltenham.

Well, Dawn Run completed the course all right, but well before the end she had unshipped her jockey, Tony Mullins. A delightful Irishman, and the son of the horse's trainer, Tony would still not be everyone's idea of a tidy steeplechase jockey, and he was unseated from both his rides in 'chases today. He was well in front on Dawn Run when horse and rider parted company, leaving the big race of the day in the hands of Misty Spirit and yours truly. I accepted the chance eagerly, but reflected later that neither the horse nor I will receive due credit for the victory. I will be amazed if we get more than a passing mention as all newspaper accounts of the race dwell on the misfortune of the great mare. Still, I've got another winner and a nice payout in my pocket; the Mullins family have to go back home to Ireland and return to the drawing-board. Who am I to moan?

Finished a good day with a Chinese meal in Baldock. A place called the Golden Rickshaw sounds authentic enough and the food is excellent, as I can testify after the latest of several visits. What I can't work out is that the manager — who is a racing nut and always finds me a table even when they are full — goes by the name of 'Wally'. Nothing very Chinese about Wally, is there?

SUNDAY 26 JANUARY

My major dilemma of an otherwise slovenly day was whether to devote my evening to the Superbowl on TV or go for my regular game of snooker. I finally opted for the American football, it being the highspot of a season I had followed so closely, but the match was so one-sided I was soon wishing I had played snooker.

The weather has altered dramatically. After what has been a pretty mild winter so far it looks as if we are in for a cold snap and the frost was so thick this morning that I can't see there being any racing at Leicester tomorrow.

MONDAY 27 AND TUESDAY 28 JANUARY

All racing has been frozen off. I am not one who chafes at having a couple of days off — I'm happy enough to laze around in front of a log fire with a good book. But the frustrating part of it is organising rides for meetings which have precious little chance of going ahead. You have to go through the motions every day, phoning up your regular trainers and confirming their plans, and if more than one or two days in succession are abandoned you know that you are in for problems, with rides you had managed to space out through the week being concertinered to a point where you have to start upsetting trainers again.

WEDNESDAY 29 JANUARY

What began as a good day and might have turned into an excellent one actually became a near-disaster for the simple reason that I broke my number one golden rule and took a ride on a novice chaser from outside my usual string of trainers. I had been lulled into it because the trainer was Roddy Armytage, highly respected and particularly successful with his young 'chasers. The horse concerned, Two Eagles, is not without ability, and was in fact going reasonably well. It wasn't his fault that he was brought down, nor was it mine, but it could easily have put me out for weeks. The first thing to hit the ground was my nose, which currently feels as if it is twice the size of the rest of my face. Then a following horse kicked me on the wrist. This was potentially much worse. For an awful few moments I believed that it was broken, such was the pain. In fact I have been lucky to escape with bruising, as much to pride as body.

Because of all this I had to give up my final ride. It didn't concern me at first. Although Young Nicholas is a very nice horse he was having his first run of the season, carrying 11 stone 11 pounds in soft ground, and Nicky Henderson assured me he had no chance. Peter Scudamore stepped in for the ride and, damn me, went and won on him. This Windsor meeting had begun so well, too. I won the handicap chase on a horse called Socks Downe, giving Jeff King his first winner of a frustrating season. But when I might have gone on to ride a double and further close the gap at the top of the championship table, I instead ended up battered and sore, not to mention having given a winner to one of my closest rivals!

My one consolation tonight is that things could be very much worse. I was only offered the ride on Two Eagles because Mr Armytage's regular jockey, Anthony Webber, is injured yet again. After the latest of a sequence of recent falls, poor 'Ant' was reported to have blood coming from his ears and nose. I fear that this game will finish him before long. Like Sam Morshead, of whom there is still no sign of a return, he is probably suffering accumulated concussion, which can get so bad that you feel dizzy for days even if you fall on your backside.

It always seems a long walk back to the weighing room after being beaten on a fancied horse. Alan Johnson

The season's greatest day. Nick and I look tense as See You Then walks out to defend his championship hurdler title

. . . striding up that long Cheltenham hill to the line

. . . the moment of truth as we tackle 'Scu' and Gaye Brief at the last

. . . and now it's all smiles as the champion returns. Caroline Norris

Every jockey I know reads the Life *like a bible – when they wake up in the morning, often at the races, and then again before bed.* Alan Johnson

Kathies Lad (RIGHT) *is still the best two-mile handicap chaser in training, and he gave me my one winner at a highly eventful Aintree meeting.* Alan Johnson

THURSDAY 30 JANUARY

It was with some relief that I woke to hear the announcement that both today's meetings had been abandoned. Often this radio bulletin — sometimes the sight of the purple printed message on the teletext service — leads to a bout of purple language from S. Smith Eccles, but this morning I was so sore — I would have struggled to ride anyway. See You Then is due to run on Saturday and I can't afford to be below par for that, so this afternoon I went into Newmarket for some ultrasound treatment on my wrist, which has stiffened up badly.

FRIDAY 31 JANUARY

Thank God. I shall be very pleased to see the back of January — never my favourite month anyway, and this year, it seems right now, the bringer of more bad tidings and bad breaks even than usual.

Nicky Henderson has twice rung up to ask if I am OK for tomorrow and although I am happy enough that the injury is nothing serious, I knew he would expect me to prove it to him at Sandown today. He is a trainer who, quite properly, will not allow his jockey to ride a top-class horse if he is anything less than 100 per cent, so my relief can well be imagined when I came through the public examination with flying colours — riding Nicky a novice chase winner on Paulatim. He did the job well but I almost made a botch of it in the closing stages. As we approached the final fence my horse was hanging into the eventual runner-up, who was alongside on my left. I knew I had to pull my whip through into my left hand and satisfy the stewards that I was doing everything to keep the horse straight, but I found the manouevre trickier than planned. The problem is that I am entirely right-handed, and although I can hold the whip in my left, and wave it about down the horse's flank, it is no more than a gesture. Somehow, I did enough to persuade Paulatim to respond and check her course, and the race was won without recourse to the stewards' room. But afterwards in the weighing-room as I joked about it with the other lads I was surprised to hear how many of them owned up to being similarly inadequate with the stick in their 'wrong hand' in a driving finish. It is

97

something every one of us practises, but not all of us can be ambidexterous!

All the top three jockeys in the table rode a winner this afternoon — Simon, after a very lean patch, celebrating his 50th of the season — so at the end of January and the start of the serious business of the campaign's major events, we are bunched up with all to play for: Sherwood 50, Scudamore 49, Smith Eccles 47. Luck and injuries will play a big part, I am sure ... but it is proving to be every bit as open a race as I predicted when the season began.

FEBRUARY

SATURDAY 1 FEBRUARY

The reputations of two equine champions were laid on the line today; both survived the public examination in very impressive style. We were at Sandown, a big day's racing on one of our biggest and plushest tracks. There is something special about this place, tucked into a green corner of stockbroker territory in plummy Esher. It is not only a highly challenging course, it also has facilities which are the envy of virtually every racetrack in the country. It has a buzzing, big-time atmosphere and, like many other jockeys who have experienced the thrill of a decent winner or two here, it figures largely among my favourite courses.

Today, though, could have been special for me on any course in England because it was the day on which I was reunited with See You Then, my chance ride and unforgettable winner in the 1985 Champion Hurdle at Cheltenham. The naked nerves of trainer Nicky Henderson, a more emotional man than me and today quite visibly tortured by anxiety as we awaited the race, were testimony to the importance of the occasion as the horse made its first competitive appearance in ten and a half months.

It was a significant day too for my pal Peter Scudamore, now with his first Gold Cup in his sights as well as his first outright jockeys' championship. The switch of jockeys on the brilliant black giant, Burrough Hill Lad, had caused considerable media controversy. Many people thought owner Stan Riley had been cruelly hasty in ditching Phil Tuck, who had after all ridden the horse to the Gold Cup two years earlier, after a couple of disappointing setbacks. But 'Scu' could not afford to waste any sympathy. He had to take a clinically professional view of a heaven-sent opportunity and simply hope that the big horse came back to his best and got to Cheltenham sound.

'The Lad' took the stage first, contesting the valuable Gains-borough Chase off top weight of 12 stone. 'Scu's' mental state may easily have been confused, because among his opponents was Run and Skip, the tiny but tenacious horse from John Spearing's Warwickshire yard, who had begun the season as a middle-of-the-road handicapper yet developed — chiefly under 'Scu's' inspired riding — into a Gold Cup candidate in his own right. It can't have been easy for Pete to desert this great servant after some marvellous wins, notably in the Welsh Grand National and in the Mildmay Chase on this Sandown course. But I felt he was doing the right thing, and the race bore me out.

I had expected to be viewing the race on TV in the weighing-room but instead I was out there on the course, having picked up the ride on the Irish-trained Rainbow Warrior when Jonjo had a bad fall in the previous event. The poor guy has suffered quite enough recently, and I feared this was another serious setback when I saw him being loaded onto a stretcher with his leg in a splint. There was relief all round when it turned out to be a case of bruising alone. At least it provided me with a decent ride and, as it turned out, a share of the prize money. I led the field into the straight for the last time, Run and Skip having lost all chance with a bad mistake at the first of the notorious 'railway fences' in the back straight. But I could sense 'Scu' simply biding his time on the 'Lad' and, sure enough, he took it up at the per-fect moment and went away to win by ten lengths.

See You Then's victory in the following race, the Oteley Hurdle, was every bit as smooth. Giving away stacks of weight to decent hurdlers such as Asir, Tom Sharp and Sabin du Loir was one of his problems; the other, potentially more serious, was that he was palpably not fully fit. He still carried plenty of condition, which was always the plan with Cheltenham still six weeks away, so I was delighted when a slow pace was set which played into my horse's hands. I came to take it up after the last and only had to push him out to win tidily by two-and-a-half lengths. I appreci-ated the relieved looks on the faces of the Henderson camp, back in the winner's enclosure!

It was, all in all, a brilliant day's racing. Although not personally involved, I relished a titanic novice chase battle between Berlin and Desert Orchid, enjoyed my close rival Simon's win on Ballinacurra Lad, and even bore the disappointment of defeat on my four-year-old hotpot, Arnhall, with no more than a pang of regret and a conviction that he will be better on good ground.

I left Sandown marvelling once again at the great quality of racing it perenially provides and saying a silent thank you to their young and efficient clerk of the course, Mark Kershaw. It is fashionable for jockeys to knock clerks and, in truth, some of them are so poor they ask for it. But in a job where people only tend to notice you when things go wrong, Mark is a great example of how things should be done. He achieved wonders today to keep racing on after a sharp frost, and he was later, as ever, courteous and helpful to trainers, jockeys and pressmen alike. I only wish there were more up to his standard.

SUNDAY 2 FEBRUARY

I made a major breakthrough in my snooker career — a break of 20! It may not sound much if you are accustomed to watching the likes of Davis and Thorburn but it meant potting six consecutive balls and to me that was the equivalent of climbing a particularly steep mountain.

MONDAY 3 FEBRUARY

That fall from Two Eagles at Windsor last week re-educated me over the merits and demerits of accepting chance rides. I could have gone to Wolverhampton today and earned 50 quid, but it was a novice chase and, set off by renewed throbbing from my wrist, the alarm bells rang in my brain. I refused the ride and stayed at home, a little poorer but very much safer, and ultimately more content.

TUESDAY 4 FEBRUARY

Luck is so important in this game, and you cannot be champion jockey without at least your fair share of it. Today, my luck was non-existent, whereas Peter Scudamore's fortunes are currently

101

flying so high that he can do no wrong. I had three booked rides at today's Warwick meeting, two of them holding a reasonable chance of winning. All three, believe it or not, were ballotted out under the Jockey Club rule which comes into play when too many horses declare for any race. One ballotted out would have been unfortunate, three was almost unbearable.

'Scu' meanwhile, had gone to yesterday's Wolverhampton meeting to ride two absolute no-hopers. Both were duly beaten out of sight. But when Graham Bradley didn't show due to an attack of food poisoning, Pete took the ride on Stearsby for Jenny Pitman and won on him. Then, with Graham McCourt absent through flu, he picked up another chance ride on King Ba Ba — and won on that one, too. You can say, of course, that he deserved the breaks because he had bothered to go there and I had stayed at home, but then that is Pete all through. I freely admit he is more thoroughly dedicated to chasing winners than I am, which in all probability means that he will be champion jockey this season, and I won't. That double yesterday has taken him to the front of the field for the first time, and both Simon and I know we have a battle on hand to knock him off the perch now. Our cause may not be helped much by the weather. This morning's newspapers gloomily predicted with what seemed total confidence a major freeze-up on the way here from Siberia. That could easily put paid to racing for a week or so.

WEDNESDAY 5 FEBRUARY

I am writing this entry a day late for a very good reason. It is now Thursday the 6th, and I have just got home from yesterday's Ascot meeting. I think this needs some detailed explanation....

9.00 a.m.

Still not sure whether I am riding at Ascot or Ludlow. The weather has begun to bite and there is an inspection at Ascot in half-an-hour. If racing goes ahead, I will be there to ride River Ceiriog for Nicky. The dilemma is that Smart Reply runs at Ludlow and will probably win, but to get there in time I will have to leave home by 9.30 a.m. I am hovering by the phone, my bag packed and ready to go.

9.30 a.m.
Still waiting. But the phone has rung twice — some good news and some bad. The bad came from Nicky, who tells me that Young Nicholas, my intended ride in the Schweppes Hurdle at Newbury on Saturday, will not now run. The good news came in a surprise call from John Spearing, offering me the ride on Run and Skip in the Gold Cup. With 'Scu' committed to Burrough Hill Lad and Sam Morshead, who rode the horse previously, still out injured, John had a headache. I was very happy to solve it for him. I also hear that Tony Mullins has been 'jocked off' Dawn Run and Jonjo will ride her at Cheltenham. I'm sorry for Tony but not surprised. I think it is the right decision — in the Gold Cup you need everything going for you; mistakes there cannot be forgiven.

9.45 a.m.
Ascot plan to inspect again at 11.00 a.m. which effectively makes my decision for me. It's a shade irritating because I am sure River Ceiriog won't win and I think Smart Reply will. But as both horses are trained by N. Henderson, I have to go where he tells me.

10.30 a.m.
Left home for Ascot. It may yet be abandoned, so I plan to stop off at Alan Jarvis's home at Royston and ring the course ... I am beginning to think I will have to buy a car phone.

12.30 p.m.
Arrive at Ascot. They have had four inspections but racing is on. It was obviously touch and go, and they have put back the first race by half-an-hour, but you have to applaud them for the effort which has clearly gone into keeping the meeting on, even if I am doing it through clenched teeth after this morning of indecision.

2.15 p.m.
River Ceiriog did not win. But he did run a blinder to take third place behind two good animals. He might be better than I thought. I have also just heard that Smart Reply was beaten at

Ludlow, so I missed nothing by having to come here. Now I need a drink.

8.00 p.m.
I have had a drink; in fact, I've had several. Peter Shilton, the England goalkeeper and an old friend, had invited me up to the Metropole Casino box at the races. As I had no further rides after the first race, I got up there early in the afternoon, which is always dangerous. One generous scotch led to another and by the time racing was over, Peter and I had acquired the taste for the stuff and so we went on to a pub in Ascot with another England footballer, Tony Woodcock. With the news that all tomorrow's racing is already off, we have now come to another decision. I am leaving my car here, good sense prevailing, and we are off up to the West End for a night out at that exclusive and expensive haunt of the famous, Tramp.

4.00 a.m.
Thursday — back at Ascot. Emerged from a thoroughly good night with the lads and found, to my great surprise, that the Siberian weather had struck while I was 'underground'. It was snowing hard and, by the time my taxi-driver had navigated back to the racecourse where I could collect my car, it was lying thick on the ground. The journey home could be interesting.

7.00 a.m.
I have reached Royston and I have had enough. The snow is bad and becoming worse by the hour. It's been very slow going, and I am whacked. Pull into a layby, flick back the reclining seat, and settle down for a welcome nap . . . .

9.00 a.m.
This is serious: I've just woken up to find the snow half-way up the car. I forced open the door and surveyed the dire truth — I am stuck.

1.00 p.m.
Home at last! Unshaven, dishevelled and exhausted, I tottered

across a field, through thick snow, to knock up a farmer and persuade him that my plight merited the use of his tractor. He relented and brought the tractor round onto the road to tow my car out of the drift. Once I was back in the centre of the road I was OK again, and managed to stay awake long enough to cover the few miles remaining of the longest journey I have ever undertaken from Ascot to Newmarket.

Today's meeting at Huntingdon was abandoned, which was really just as well — I don't think I would have been in a state to do myself justice even if I had got to the course on time! The entire country, I hear, is now blanketted in snow — and I'm off to bed.

SATURDAY 8 FEBRUARY
Racing has ground to a halt. The freeze-up is every bit as bad as the forecasters promised and I, for one, have come to the conclusion that it will be at least another week before we have a chance of resuming. So, on impulse, I am going to grab that holiday I have been hankering after for so long. I considered a return to Barbados, which would certainly be pleasantly warm, but finally rejected the idea in favour of a skiing trip to France. I've never been before, which is one very good reason for trying it in my book, and I have to say I am also attracted by the tales of hectic apres-ski which filter back through friends of mine who are regular winter sports fans. So today I have been on the telephone trying to round up a suitable team for the expedition. One unexpected refusal came from J. Francome. In years gone by he would have not needed a second bidding — he would have been with us like a shot. I don't know whether he is finding the pressures of training getting on top of him or whether he is just getting old!

SUNDAY 9 FEBRUARY
The weather continues to be desperate and, on the basis that there is no time like the present, we are booked to fly out of Gatwick this afternoon for a week on the piste. My skiing squad is a bare three — Paul Barton, Oliver Sherwood and myself. To my great chagrin, I discovered that Oliver's brother Simon has

already gone on a separate skiing holiday without telling me. I shall be having words with him when I see him.

I have no regrets at all about leaving England in February. It is a cheerless, tedious month in which there is little pleasure to be had from racing even when it survives the weather. Even the cancellation of yesterday's big meeting at Newbury caused me to shed no tears, although I do have a certain sympathy with Schweppes, whose sponsorship of the big handicap hurdle at Newbury looks a dubious investment — it has now been lost to the weather four times in the past six years. The three holiday-makers drove down to Gatwick for an afternoon flight to Italy, followed by a long but picturesque coach ride into the mountains and on to the French border. It was late when we arrived at the hotel and I admit to just a slight pang of doubt about the week to come. What if I break my leg, with Cheltenham a month away? I put it quickly out of my mind and turned my attentions to the matter in hand. Racing, I vowed, would remain firmly at the back of my thoughts for this rare week of escapism.

SUNDAY 16 FEBRUARY
We landed at Gatwick hale and healthy. The week passed rapidly and, at times, riotously. I never thought there could be anything to compare with the thrill of riding good horses over fences but I now admit that skiing at speed rivals it. It was pure exhilaration, hard work now and again but great fun throughout; and thank-fully, none of us sustained anything more lasting than the odd bruise. Even my tortured, temperamental knee stood up to the unaccustomed strain very well until our final afternoon, when a few jolting pains reminded me of my infirmity. The skiing crowd is certainly a change from the racing fraternity I mix with every day of the ten-month season and, interestingly, the three of us hardly talked shop at all. I think each one of us was grateful for the chance of a mid-winter break in which the season's stresses and strains, highs and lows, could temporarily be pigeon-holed.

Immersed in the day-to-day routine of the long racing campaign, it is all too easy to cut adrift from the reality of the outside world. To a certain extent, racing folk live a cocooned existence, mixing chiefly with their own kind and spending virtually all their waking hours doing something connected with their job. It is a peculiar lifestyle. I have no great desire to change it, as I still consider myself fortunate to be well paid for doing something I love. But it has to be said that racing can become almost incestuous in its atmosphere and the occasional week, entirely divorced from thoughts of runners and riders, horses and handicaps, restores a healthy balance to a dangerously one-track mind.

It occurs to me, driving home tonight, that it ought to be possible to make this an annual winter break — God knows, the British February is usually dire enough to allow at least a week's escape with barely a missed meeting; already I have enlisted the support of Paul and Oliver for a repeat performance in 1987, and we have opted for Austria for our next venture.

TUESDAY 18 FEBRUARY
Having craved all season for a holiday, and finally got one, I now need a rest to get over it. I'm just about recovered now, two days after arriving home!

The weather has still not broken, nor is there any immediate prospect of it doing so. Nightly TV forecasts from the mournful Michael Fish or the manic Ian McGaskill follow a tediously similar pattern; the isobars seem unchanged from day to day and no-one can predict when any remotely warmer air might be able to force a path into the country.

Everyone in racing faces certain problems during a prolonged break such as this. Some face considerably more than others. I am among the more fortunate, in that I make enough money while the weather is fair to survive an enforced holiday of a few weeks; I even welcome it at first, although I am prepared to admit it will not be long before the novelty of free time wears thin. But in jump racing only a dozen or so of the jockeys are in this category; the vast majority, the middle-of-the-road boys who scratch around for their daily riding fee and the scores of young hopefuls trying to make their way in the game, can get into quite serious hardship if a freeze lasts much beyond a week or two. A few have outside jobs which sustain them and others are attached to stables — but even for them, the prospect of riding out two lots every

107

morning with the temperature ten degrees below freezing is an unenviable way of making a few quid.

The trainers have a different kind of headache. Although the lack of racing can hit their pocket as it means there is no prize money going into the pot, they are at least still receiving their weekly training fees from the frustrated owners who cannot run their horses. But it is the trainer's responsibility to keep those horses as fit as possible during bad weather, and when the freeze bites as deeply as it has done now, that can be an awesome task. For some, set in the bleakest and worst-hit parts of the country and lacking the plush indoor or all-weather facilities owned by their luckier neighbours, it is pretty near impossible and there will inevitably be some plump and unfit horses appearing when racing eventually does resume. With that in mind, I was relieved and delighted to hear that my retaining trainer, Nicky Henderson, has discovered an arduous but effective method of ensuring his string is kept on the go, come what may.

Nicky has an all-weather paddock in his Lambourn yard, but the term 'all-weather' is in this case inapplicable. Even such surfaces as that cannot cope with constant temperatures well below zero and Nicky soon discovered that the paddock froze solid each night and was quite unusable at exercise time in the morning. There was only one way to overcome that and I must say I would have found it distinctly unappealing. But my guv'nor is an extremely dedicated trainer so, every two hours, through the night and every night, a tractor and harrow is driven around the paddock to keep it loose and functional. Various members of the Henderson staff take their shifts, but I happen to know Nicky is shouldering a good deal of this bleak and unpleasant task himself. It obviously works, too, as he informed me today that the group of horses he is particularly anxious to keep fit have not missed a day's exercise since the weather took its icy grip on the country. See You Then is reported to be in good shape, although we are all obviously hoping to get another race into him before the Champion Hurdle.

SUNDAY 23 FEBRUARY
Boredom has set in. There is not the slightest change in the

weather, the long-range forecast is equally grim and S. Smith Eccles is becoming more irritable by the day. Those around me, and especially Di, are, I am afraid, beginning to feel the sharp edge of my tongue as the tedious days drag on. I have virtually given up reading the *Sporting Life* now, as the four-day declarations which are still appearing daily for the forthcoming scheduled meetings mean nothing when they have precisely no chance of ever being run. I speak to Nicky regularly, but there seems little point in phoning even the other trainers who habitually give me rides. They have enough to think about in these circumstances without having a frustrated jockey moaning down the telephone.

If things were different I could enjoy the scene outside. Snailwell, the tiny hamlet where we moved into an old cottage a little over a year ago, is a charming sight for anyone interested in photographing typically English winter scenes. I can just picture it on the front of a postcard. The village is protected from further building and so its character is much as it has always been; the Snailwell Stud surrounds it, and the facilities for inhabitants extend to one pub, but no shops. Out in my garden there is a well from where the villagers once drew their daily supplies of water. A good job they don't still have to do so — they would need a pick-axe to break up the ice each day!

Even the ducks and chickens I keep are looking miserable, no doubt feeling the chilly pinch through their feathers. I am keeping them well fed but, unfortunately, I am also eating rather too heavily myself. Boredom is the reason, of course — with so little else to occupy me, I am picking at food in a way I would never do when I am busy racing. Although I am riding out for Di on the odd occasion, it is not enough to keep the flab at bay and I fear I am now about five pounds heavier than I should be; something will have to be done.

THURSDAY 27 FEBRUARY

Three weeks have now elapsed since the last racing in Britain and I would wager there is not a jockey or trainer in the country who is not champing at the bit for a resumption. The most appalling thought of all is that the Cheltenham Festival is now less than a fortnight away, and it is going to need a fairly rapid and complete thaw to allow that meeting — the biggest of the season for all of us involved — to escape the unthinkable fate of joining the list of abandonments. And that thaw still looks a long way off as I gaze out of the window in my snug, normally just a hideaway room on Sundays or when I want an hour alone in the evening but, just recently, almost a permanent residence.

It is small consolation, but right now there is at least nothing to stand in the way of social engagements and, yesterday, for the first time in years, I was able to accept an invitation to the William Hill Golden Spurs luncheon in London. Season after season, I have had to decline through a clash with riding commitments, but as the Worcester meeting had inevitably been called off days ago, I joined a strikingly large contingent of jumping people, all relieving the tedium besetting us all. From there, I went on to the opening of a new restaurant in St James's called Silks which, as you may gather, has a racing theme. A pleasant day, but another which did nothing for the ever-increasing amount of overweight I am carrying.

FRIDAY 28 FEBRUARY

My month's work consisted of just four rides and one winner — on that long-ago opening day of February at Sandown. Today's abandonments have brought the total number of meetings lost this season up to 104, closing fast on the record of 136 which was established in the 1967-68 winter. It is enough to turn any man to drink — but unfortunately I can't even take that option. I am now in strict training. On the possibly absurd assumption that the weather will relent in time for Cheltenham I am determined to get back into decent physical shape and get some idle muscles working again.

I have started a diet, which chiefly revolves around exercising some self-discipline and keeping off the biscuits and chocolate I had taken to chomping between the more serious meals. Bread and potatoes are also strictly rationed from now on. I have decided to start running regularly and so, this morning, well wrapped up against another raw day, I set off jogging around the Suffolk lanes. As my boredom threshold is lower than most, however, I quickly get fed up with the tedious plod of a run and so I took a football with me to kick around on the fields and footpaths as a distraction. Tonight, I am continuing my exercise kick — by playing a game of snooker. . . .

MARCH

SATURDAY 1 MARCH

Panic is descending on the ranks of National Hunt trainers. Cheltenham is now just ten days away and we woke up this morning to the sight of a fresh and intense blizzard. It is the fourth consecutive Saturday without racing and although Messrs Fish and McGaskill are now hinting vaguely that the middle of next week could see a temporary end to this wretched spell, even that would give the ground scant time to thaw completely, and the poor trainers no time at all to get any racecourse work into their Cheltenham horses.

SUNDAY 2 MARCH

Spent the morning checking and confirming my Cheltenham races, keeping my fingers firmly crossed for the weather. I currently have ten engaged rides over the three days, which means there are only four races, open to professionals, in which I am still free. The Smith Eccles squad looks very promising, too.

I have expanded my training programme to include riding out two lots each morning for Di. I still feel podgy, but my dedication did not extend to going without Sunday lunch. I downed it ravenously with the silent promise that it would be my final treat before the Festival.

This evening was spent in mourning. After all these months of snooker practice, I have suddenly lost my partner. Tommy Keddie, one of my oldest and dearest pals, is leaving town and going to drive trucks for his sister's haulage firm in Carlisle. Tommy and I go back to my early days in Newmarket when we both came here as raw-boned wide-eyed teenagers from working-class backgrounds. That was 14 years back, yet still I have a vivid memory of turning up at my first 'digs' and finding myself allotted to a room smaller than my current kitchen — and I had to share that room with five other lads. Three sets of bunk beds were squeezed into the box-room and us half-dozen innocents, all thrust into stable-work without really knowing what to expect or where it would take us, had to make do and get along with each other.

Coming straight from a comfortable home and a close-knit family, it came as a major shock to me and after three nights in 'digs' I almost packed my bags and caught the bus home. I often wonder what would have happened to me if I had given up at that point. Would I have ended up following my father and my other ancestors, going daily down a Derbyshire coalmine? Somehow I can't imagine it. I have been down the pit just once, when, later in my apprenticeship, I had a weekend at home and my father took me down to show me what I was missing. I don't mind admitting it frightened me — and we ventured nowhere near the deepest interior, the part where Dad said he would often spend hours on his stomach, hacking at the coalface in incredibly claustrophobic conditions. No, I don't think I was made to be a miner ... but then Tommy Keddie, after all these years in Newmarket, has gone back to *his* roots. It makes me realise how lucky I am. But I'm still short of a snooker partner!

MONDAY 3 MARCH
Another sharp frost this morning, but unless I am engaging in entirely wishful thinking, I swear it is now appreciably milder than it has been for weeks. Shall I chance another run before my sparse supper?

TUESDAY 4 MARCH
This morning I felt like the kid waking up on Christmas Day to find that Santa really has left a sackful of presents at the foot of the bed. My usual wary peer through the curtains produced a sight which at first I refused to accept. But after blinking sharply, rubbing my eyes and staring once more, I had to believe it — it was pouring with rain! What's more, it has rained for most of the

day, taking at least some of the frost out of the long-suffering ground.

I celebrated by getting back into a racing mood. After riding out, I went to take part in a video being made by Ladbrokes, chatting about my Cheltenham rides and their chances. Now that TV is allowed in betting shops, I can just imagine the scene next Tuesday lunchtime; the punters glued to this video, drinking in the confident thoughts of jockeys like me. What they may not realise is that jockeys as a breed are some of the worst tipsters in the game!

WEDNESDAY 5 MARCH

Racing in Britain resumes after an absence of exactly one month — the trouble is, the surviving meeting happens to be at Catterick, way up the A1 in the north of Yorkshire and foreign soil to us southern jockeys. So I endured yet another day off, but at least the thaw does seem to have begun in earnest. There is still a good bit of frost hanging around, most particularly in the south, and we may not resume racing down here until the weekend. But the long-range forecast is encouraging for Cheltenham which, after all this time twiddling our thumbs, is all that really matters.

After riding out this morning I popped into Gavin Pritchard-Gordon's Newmarket home for a bite of breakfast. The chat got around to the subject of trying to keep fit during the bad weather and when I told Gav of my excess poundage he beckoned me downstairs and showed me what looked like a half-built canoe! A rowing machine, he told me, is the ideal way to stay fit. I tried it out for five minutes and saw exactly what he meant. As I creaked to my feet every muscle in my body ached and it came home to me just how much of an effect enforced idleness can have. Impetuous as ever, I decided on the spot that I would go out and buy one of these machines, which certainly appear (by the area of aches) to get muscles in the stomach, back and legs working in unison. I can set it up in a spare room and install a tape player so that the music saves me from giving up too soon through boredom.

THURSDAY 6 MARCH

Another slight frost this morning retarded the thawing process a shade and put paid to today's two scheduled meetings, but it was still a day of big racing news, dominated by the story that, for the second year running, Burrough Hill Lad is a late withdrawal from the Gold Cup. He had been promoted to favourite after his win at Sandown and, among those supposedly in the know, was widely expected to repeat his 1984 win. But, just as he did last year, the big horse has suffered an untimely training setback — on this occasion, apparently the result of working on the beach at Burnham. Beach work is favoured only by a proportion of trainers during a freeze-up; there are those who regard it as a high-risk surface on which horses are all too likely to break down. This incident is bound to refuel the debate.

My first feeling on hearing the news was one of self-preservation. This may sound odd, but let me explain. The story of Burrough Hill Lad was actually related to me over the telephone, by David Nicholson. Although nothing was said directly, I suspected that David was phoning to sound me out over the prospect of Peter Scudamore — now without his Gold Cup ride — reclaiming the engagement for Run and Skip. It wasn't long later that the phone began to ring in earnest, with pressmen wanting to know if I was still riding the Spearing candidate. At six this evening I finally received the call I had been expecting. It was 'Scu'. I told him that I had accepted the ride on an understanding with John Spearing that I would keep it, whatever may befall Burrough Hill Lad. 'Scu' told me he already knew this, having spoken to Mr Spearing himself.

The trainer's solution had apparently been to inform 'Scu' that he must sort it out with me. Now, Pete is a good mate of mine and I didn't blame him for trying to get the ride back but I also had no intention of backing down. 'What would you do in my position?' I asked him, and he immediately knew he was chasing a lost cause.

A couple of hours later, after several more newspaper calls, I was cheered up when Jeff McCarthy, one of Run and Skip's owners, rang up himself. He rapidly banished my sense of foreboding over what he was about to say by insisting: 'As far as we are concerned, you will ride the horse. Take no notice of the speculation to the contrary.' I give him and his colleagues full marks for loyalty. 'Scu' has won some big races for them, and I knew more than a few owners who would have been utterly unscrupulous in these circumstances, but these guys know the terms on which I was booked and they are standing by them. For my part, I have to go to Stratford racecourse on Sunday morning to ride Run and Skip a piece of work and then watch some videos of his recent races. That is a small price to pay for the privilege of a Gold Cup ride on a horse now down to 10-1 third favourite. Tonight, for the first time, it occurred to me that I have a genuine chance of becoming the first jockey to ride the Gold Cup and Champion Hurdle double at the Festival meeting.

FRIDAY MARCH 7
My first ride in a month — and I had to go to the relative wilds of Market Rasen for it! With Sandown frozen off, I was keen to get my eye back in with a spin on something, so I took the ride on a little hurdler for Newmarket trainer Gerry Blum at the Lincolnshire track. I don't go there very often, although it is not a difficult journey, and after riding out for Di this morning I was glad I had taken the decision. I schooled one horse for her and then had a real blow. I was exhausted! I've been running, I've worked at my diet and now I've even got a rowing machine — but nothing keeps a jockey fit like race-riding, and I knew then that there would be some very tired riders going round at Market Rasen.

The course was in an awful state — like a ploughed field — and one of the bends was positively dangerous. But I still came away with a sense of having achieved something. My horse didn't win — finished third, in fact — but like a cricketer reporting back after the winter break, I have had my first innings and I feel more confident for it.

SATURDAY 8 MARCH
This game can mock you all too often. Us professional jockeys, kicking our heels for a month and now anxious to make an impression again, were all upstaged today by one Mr Gerald Oxley, gentleman amateur rider. Gerald was partnering the Queen Mother's Special Cargo in the Horse and Hound's Grand Military Gold Cup, salvaged from yesterday's abandoned card

and run as the first race today. Now, this race is restricted to amateurs who have served in a branch of the armed forces and it often provides some memorably unorthodox styles, but there was nothing wrong with Mr Oxley's performance. At the last fence on the far side, three from home, his leathers broke, and he was obliged to see out the business end of the race with his legs swinging down the horse's neck. Undeterred, he somehow conjured a late burst from Special Cargo to get up on the line and win. It was an effort of which any top professional would have been proud.

I managed nothing remotely as memorable. The decisive factor, when racing resumes after such a lengthy break, is how much work your trainers have managed to get into their horses, and the three I rode today all 'blew up'. Two were for Jeff King, who is based on the Marlborough Downs and has obviously had problems keeping his string going. The one thing which did greatly please me, however, was my weight — I managed to do 10 stone 3 pounds quite comfortably.

I stayed the night with the Francomes and did nothing very extravagent. In fact, we played Trivial Pursuits. I did not win . . . .

SUNDAY 9 MARCH
An early start, on the road to John Spearing's yard just west of Stratford. Run and Skip has never struck me as a very handsome animal to look at and today the impression was amplified. He does not even give a great feel when first you sit on him, but his recent record bears no criticism. In each race he has run, his bravery and wholehearted enthusiasm for the game has shone through, and if there will inevitably be more gifted horses in Thursday's Gold Cup field, I can't believe there will be any who outdo my fellow for sheer effort.

After riding a piece of work on him I was shown video recordings of his major races this season. Although I had ridden in most of the races, one is always far more concerned with one's current mount than any other horse and this was certainly an instructive session. The horse, I know, likes to be up with the pace all the way, and it will be fascinating to take part in a duel for the lead with Dawn Run!

Back home by lunchtime, I made some calls to trainers simply

117

to reconfirm my Cheltenham rides. I was pleased with the result and now, after weeks of inactivity and a growing belief that the big meeting would not take place, the adrenalin is beginning to flow for what is always the biggest week of my year.

MONDAY 10 MARCH

There was a time when I didn't believe in caution. Not any more. Today, I declined all offers to go to the meeting at rustic old Southwell and occupied the time at home with a couple of lengthy sessions on my newly-acquired rowing machine.

Southwell on a Monday is rarely an appetising prospect, inevitably combining bad horses with a dodgy track, and with Cheltenham now 24 hours away, I considered it would have been madness to risk an injury which could put me out of the festival. Mind you, as I say, I have not always been so prim and sensible. Ten years ago, when I was a silly young boy, I took a spare ride in a chase at this very Southwell meeting and, of course, the thing fell. I cracked my collarbone but somehow managed to ride my Cheltenham horses, heavily strapped and dosed up with painkilling drugs. On the Wednesday, I rode Sweet Joe in the Sun Alliance Chase and by the time the race began my latest injection had worn off and I was gritting my teeth against the pain. Sweet Joe won, the first big winner of my career, but in the midst of the celebrations I silently accepted that a painful lesson had been learned. Nowadays, I avoid riding the day before Cheltenham unless one of my regular trainers has a hurdler he fancies — and then, although it is hard to refuse to ride, I go in some trepidation. Cheltenham means that much to me.

I have also come to believe that the great Festival races are best watched from a seat in the weighing-room, while sipping a cup of tea, if you do not have a decent ride offered. The days are gone when I could get any kick out of riding a no-hoper among class horses at this meeting, so I am not at all dismayed to have just the two rides tomorrow, both of which are for Nick Henderson. The first is River Ceiriog, a nice sort of novice but still a maiden and most unlikely to cut much ice in the opening event of the meeting, the Waterford Crystal Supreme Novices Hurdle. His most recent race, at Ascot last month, was his best yet, but I shall be more than happy if he runs well and finishes in the first six or seven. But then, of course, there is See You Then . . . .

I have no doubts whatever that he is the best hurdler in training and that, given the necessary luck in running, he will win the 'Champion' for the second year running. But I have to admit to being horrified when I turned on Channel Four's Teletext service at lunchtime and discovered that he is one of 24 horses declared for the race, making it the biggest Champion Hurdle field since 1964. Included in the number are a few who have no right to be taking part — mediocre horses, even a novice or two among them, whose participation in the most prestigious hurdle race of the year can only be designed to give their owners something to swank about to their chums. I believe the conditions of the race should be better framed to prevent such anomalies in the future, but as for tomorrow, my biggest worry in the race will simply be in trying to keep out of their way and steer See You Then a clear path. If I can negotiate that problem, I shall be a very disappointed man if he gets beaten.

TUESDAY 11 MARCH

Nobody in the county of Gloucestershire is more amazed or delighted tonight than yours truly. See You Then is once more the champion hurdler, which is an enormous relief, and River Ceiriog is the champion two-mile novice, which is little short of a miracle. It has been a fantastic day, quite one of the best of my career, and it has also been a very long day.

Nick had asked me to school Prime Oats, our Triumph Hurdle fancy, in Lambourn this morning before driving on to the course. I made the mistake of electing to set off in the early hours rather than driving down at my leisure last night, and so it was that, shortly after five this morning, I was poking my Mercedes tentatively through thick fog at the start of the long cross-country drive. My frustrations turned to temper as the murk persisted for much of the journey, but somehow I pulled into the drive at Windsor House in time to go out with Nick's first lot, a little chastened but otherwise none the worse for the experience.

I popped Prime Oats over some hurdles on the schooling grounds, a worthwhile exercise as he turned out to be a bit rusty, and then I worked Green Bramble, who felt in very good order for his bid to win the Ritz Club three-mile chase on Thursday — he might well have won last year at the Festival but for falling at the second last when in front, and although he has been out of sorts for much of this season, there seemed to be very little wrong with him this morning.

On the way back from the downs I saw Fred Winter, who wished me luck for the Champion Hurdle and asked if I was suffering from butterflies. I was able to tell him with complete honesty that I felt quite calm about the whole thing. Nerves, I know, affect different people in very different ways, but apart from feeling a bit shaky before my first-ever ride in the Grand National, they have rarely affected me at all. Even though I was acutely aware of the importance of the day, and although the adrenalin was pumping that shade more strongly than usual, I had none of the doubts, the fright and the apprehension which afflicts a really nervous person. Now Nick is a different story — naturally restless and a born worrier, I was in no doubt about his state this morning and I did not attempt to discuss much with him other than the races immediately ahead.

Arriving at Prestbury Park on the opening day of the Festival is always a moment of supreme anticipation. The three days' biggest jump racing on the calendar lies ahead, days in which the hopes and dreams which have been nurtured for months beforehand will either come to fruition or be dashed into deflating disappointment. Very often, of course, the expectation far outweighs the reality — so Tuesday morning is a time to savour.

Today, the crowds seemed bigger than ever, the tented village had certainly sprouted another river of tarpaulin since last year but the atmosphere was just the same as ever — exciting, intoxicating, with just a hint of Irish madness attached. I had arrived early to be sure of avoiding the worst of the traffic and I sipped tea in the weighing-room after changing into the colours of Mr Bobby McAlpine, owner of River Ceiriog, for the first event of the meeting.

If I state that the race amazed me I am not doing it justice: it was quite unbelievable. With the usual maximum field of novices, I intended to give my horse some daylight and keep him up with the pace, a plan I carried out entirely to my satisfaction. At the top of the hill I hit the front, increasingly delighted with the way he had run, yet fully expecting him to weaken rapidly after the second last.

120

Frankly, I could not have been more than slightly disappointed if he had done so, after running well for so far. But River Ceiriog was not going to fold up.

Turning into the straight we were still in front, and as we approached the last I risked a look over my shoulder, still in my heart believing that one of the well-backed hotpots would be cruising upsides to take it off me. But that one glance was enough to tell me that nothing was travelling more sweetly than me. I returned my gaze straight ahead, my heart momentarily in my mouth at that familiar but ever formidable sight of the famous hill looming ahead. But plainly it troubled me more than the horse; River Ceiriog just lengthened his stride, flew the last and stormed up the run-in to win unchallenged.

What happened back in the unsaddling enclosure is something of a blur. I remember there being relative silence as we walked in, which can only be because nobody in the vicinity had availed themselves of the 40-1 which now suddenly seemed absurdly generous. I also remember the stunned look on the guv'nor's face, and the fact that he was virtually speechless — as indeed we all were. I don't remember much else! In looking forward to Cheltenham I had set my sights on winning the Champion Hurdle and regarding any other winner as a tremendous bonus. The last thing I had planned for was to receive the bonus before the big race!

Very soon, my thoughts had turned once more to See You Then. I donned the green and white check silks and strolled out once more to the parade ring, where the terraces were now packed to bursting point with eager punters. My first sight of the horse was, I can now confess, a little alarming. He had had just the one run this season, shortly before the freeze-up, and to me he still looked on the tubby side of fit. I consoled myself with the thought that Nick had kept him constantly on the go, and would hardly be likely to have left him short of work, and kept my worries to myself.

The race itself, however, gave me no worries at all. I managed to keep See You Then clear of the pack, cruised up behind Gaye Brief going to the last and let him sprint away up the hill with that devastating turn of foot which marks him as a true champion.

121

There was never a moment when I was anything but convinced we would win, and it all went absolutely as we had planned. It was the perfect way to ride my 50th winner of the season and, not having any further rides to worry about, I was able to sample a little celebration champagne.

The most remarkable fact to emerge from my two races is that River Ceiriog covered the two miles in a time two seconds faster than See You Then, an astonishing performance for a horse who came here today as a maiden. Days like this don't happen very often and, when they do, I never want them to end. I was sensible tonight, just enjoying a couple of drinks and then a bite to eat before going back to the cottage Di and I have rented for the week in Condicote, near David Nicholson's yard and Peter Scudamore's home. I thought of them both as I pulled in — here am I with two winners on the opening day of the meeting, while 'the Duke' has never trained a single Festival winner and 'Scu' has never ridden one. I hope their luck changes.

WEDNESDAY 12 MARCH
What could possibly follow the events of the opening day? I am realistic, if nothing else, and I was not looking for any more miracles. When I woke this morning and surveyed the day's card I reached the conclusion that I had four good, worthwhile rides but that I would be hard-pushed to ride another winner. And so it proved. My reservations were as follows: Pikes Peak, who ran in the two-and-a-half mile Sun Alliance Novices Hurdle, is a potentially high-class horse, but would prefer the ground softer; Kathies Lad, in the Queen Mother Champion Chase was taking on the very best two-mile chasers from Britain and Ireland, and looked likely to be just outclassed; Highland Gold, trained by 'Ginger' McCain, was one of 32 handicap hurdlers declared for the marathon Coral Final which is annually the most difficult race of the meeting in which to find the winner; and Classified, now ten and one of Nick's most faithful servants, was going for the Mildmay of Flete Chase not completely wound up. The National is his objective and the stable had a more fancied runner in the Mildmay, the Tsarevich, which duly won for the second successive year to give Nick his third winner in two days.

Although my assessment turned out to be correct, however, I was far from disappointed with any of my horses. Pikes Peak galloped on bravely to be second and Kathies Lad — despite not looking properly fit in the paddock — ran a blinder behind Buck House and Very Promising. I hope Alan Jarvis takes him back to Liverpool, where I think he can win again.

One of the great gambles of the meeting came off today when Motivator won the Coral final for Newmarket trainer Mick Ryan and his flamboyant main owner, financier Terry Ramsden. Never a man to hide his light under a bushel, Mr Ramsden had been boasting about this horse for some time; today, not being short of readies, he put his money where his mouth is and collected the interest. The Irish, by contrast, have been suffering terribly. When Omerta won the amateur riders' chase, the fifth event on today's card, it was their first success of the meeting, and I imagine it probably came too late to save quite a number of empty wallets among the hordes who invade across the Irish Sea. For me, the Irish people make Cheltenham week what it is, and while I am very much against them running off with too many of our prizes I was actually quite pleased when they had a winner . . . especially as it was only an amateur's race!

Cheltenham being where it is, in the centre of England, most jockeys travel home each night. I am one of the few to stay in the area, but I am more and more convinced it is a good move, especially to have a cottage away from the frenzy which overtakes Cheltenham's town hotels each night of this crazy week. I went back to Condicote tonight feeling relaxed and well, and if I don't win the Gold Cup tomorrow it will not be through any fault in my preparation.

THURSDAY 13 MARCH
By 11.30, almost three hours before first-race time, a queue of cars snaked away from the course and back towards Winchcombe, to the east, and Gloucester and the M5, to the west. It was a sight to warm the heart of anyone involved in jump racing, but I must say I was glad I hadn't taken a chance on arriving an hour later.

The atmosphere was absolutely electric, as it always is on

123

Gold Cup day. If the first two days attracted record crowds, I can only imagine today's was an all-time high for the final day — almost twice the number that were here either on Tuesday or Wednesday.

On the short drive in from Condicote I mulled over my rides and decided that all four could be fancied. But, without wishing to be negative, I just could not imagine Run and Skip winning the Gold Cup. The way I saw it was this: Dawn Run had the speed and the class, but her jumping was suspect. If she jumped round, she would win; if not, I expected last season's winner Forgive 'n' Forget to triumph again, as I had heard some very good reports of him earlier in the week. That did not mean I would not be in there trying my best, but deep down I thought a place was the best I could hope for.

Paradoxically, I felt my best chance of another winner was with the least experienced of my four rides. Prime Oats had got into the Triumph Hurdle field despite still being a maiden and I gave him a really decent chance of upsetting the form horses. That, however, was one which did not work out to plan. I finished in the pack, Prime Oats showing us that he was still a shade more backward than we had hoped, and the race was won by a rank outsider in Solar Cloud — trained by David Nicholson and ridden by Peter Scudamore.

If I could not win the race myself, I considered this the ideal result, I know a little of the torment, not to mention the teasing, that these two guys have been through, as the years have totted up and their Festival winner tally has remained rooted at nil. 'Scu', in particular, had ridden a phenomenal amount of runners-up, and he must have feared he was in for another one here. Having virtually pinched the race by kicking on down the hill, Solar Cloud was rapidly coming back to the chasing field on the long, exhausting run-in, and it took all Pete's renowned finishing strength to get him home, accompanied by a totally understandable clenched fist from an exultant jockey. The enclosure was an emotional place after this overdue victory for the local stable and, back in the weighing-room, a beaming 'Scu' was showered with some very sincere congratulations.

We professionals had some time to catch our breath while the

Foxhunters Chase was run, and then we were out for the Gold Cup, which was a race I doubt I shall ever forget. If there has ever been a better or more spectacular Gold Cup I would love to see it — this one was simply a privilege to have taken part in. That Dawn Run won — becoming the first horse ever to complete the double of Champion Hurdle and Gold Cup — is part of history, while the race itself is, I am sure, engraved on the memory of at least four jockeys — Jonjo O'Neill, who rode the winner, Graham Bradley (Wayward Lad), Mark Dwyer (Forgive 'n' Forget) and myself.

My plan had been to take Dawn Run on at the head of affairs and try to force her into mistakes. This made for a strong gallop and some pretty thrilling racing from the off, and it seemed to me that the plan had worked when I caught sight of Jonjo apparently struggling with the mare as we hit the top of the hill for the final time. The trouble is, neither J.J. O'Neill nor Dawn Run ever know when they are beaten.

My horse was still in front three from home. At the second last he hit the top of the fence, halting his rhythm, but it was then that I experienced the marvellous courage of Run and Skip. He may have begun the season as a mere handicapper, but he was showing the world now that he was perfectly entitled to his place in this Gold Cup field. He plugged on bravely, and if the three-horse drama a few yards in front of him deservedly took the glory, I could have asked no more from my horse.

Those who have seen one of the countless TV repeats of the race will know that Dawn Run came back when the race looked lost, touching off Wayward Lad on the line. What followed will go down in Festival history as the most extraordinary scene ever witnessed in the winners' enclosure. There had been a form of pandemonium two years earlier, when Dawn Run won the Champion Hurdle, but that was vicarage tea-party stuff compared to this wild cavorting invasion by hundreds and hundreds of exuberant Irishmen. Jonjo was lifted high on their shoulders, then Tony Mullins, the deposed jockey yet still very much part of the Dawn Run team, received the treatment. I have never seen a racing crowd respond like that to any winner and I doubt if I shall see its like again.

There just had to be an anti-climax, of course, and it came in a manner which I suppose I could have predicted with the enigmatic Green Bramble falling at the last in the Ritz Club Chase and giving me a bruising which cost me my final ride of the meeting. He had run a good race but he was out of contention when he came down — the race was won by the Scudamore-Nicholson team, now making up for lost time.

If the day closed on a painful and disappointing note, this has still been a marvellously memorable Festival. Anyone who rides two winners at Cheltenham has to be very satisfied, especially when they include the Champion Hurdle, and I have been lucky to have some great losing rides, too. Tonight, I think, I might break out of my self-imposed chains and let my hair down. . . .

FRIDAY 14 MARCH

I began the day with a hangover, an unsurprising relic of a night when quite a few refugees from Cheltenham cut loose. I drank some farewell toasts to my pals from Ireland, and generally had a good time. After looking a good thing to win the Ritz Club award as top jockey at the meeting for the second successive season I had lost out — to 'Scu' — because he had ridden more seconds than I had (we kid him that he's a seconds specialist at Cheltenham, but that may have to change now). But that was only a minor setback to a week which gave me ample cause to celebrate.

Today brought the inevitable anti-climax. It happens every year and it is never any easier to handle. All through the winter, the racing talk is of Cheltenham. It arrives with a thumping of drums and pumping adrenalin, it holds everyone involved on an emotional high, then all too quickly it is over and the realisation that there is a full year to wait for the next Festival — and an awful lot of mediocre racing to get through — bursts the bubble in which we have all existed. Very often, I have come down to earth at Wolverhampton, riding a moderate novice on a murky Friday afternoon with a dull-faced crowd of no more than a few hundred looking on. Today, at least the scenery was better at Lingfield Park, the rural Surrey course they advertise with good reason as 'Lovely Lingfield'. I had a quiet day — a third-place being my nearest bid for a winner — and opted to stay down for tomorrow's

126

meeting on the same track rather than dragging myself back to Newmarket.

One sad piece of news punctuated an otherwise forgettable day. Anthony Webber has been forced to retire, on doctor's orders, after taking one too many bangs on the head. It is obviously the right thing to do, but I always have sympathy for a jockey of Anthony's visible enthusiasm when his retirement is dictated rather than planned. He was never the most stylish rider of my generation but he was bloody effective, and a good number of trainers will miss him.

SATURDAY 15 MARCH

Peter Scudamore rode four winners at Chepstow today, convincing me that he will be champion jockey if he stays fit until the end of the season. I know this may sound like another slice of defeatism — it was not all that long ago that I was resigning myself to Simon Sherwood taking the title — but if nothing else, I am a hard realist about my own shortcomings and I totally accept that 'Scu' is prepared to work harder at this game than I am.

It would not always have been this way. Time was when I would go anywhere for a ride, be it the dodgiest novice chaser in the book or the best hurdler in the country. I took no account of risks and paid no heed to the luxuries of life. But I have been going round a good few years now and I have seen a lot more of life, both inside and outside racing. It is no longer attractive to me to earn £50 to ride a horse which has an even-money chance of decanting me at the first fence, with all the painful ramifications that may have. When I take a ride from outside my retaining stable, I want to get on that horse thinking it has at least some chance of winning — and then I will give it everything.

'Scu' is a few years younger than me. He is also hungrier for success. Winning the championship, as a specific entity, must mean more to him than it does to me because it seems he is prepared to be on the phone for hours at a time every evening in an attempt to book a ride in every race at the meeting he goes to. He will many times ring up trainers he doesn't know and others he has never taken a ride for, in the constant quest for winners. I am not saying he is wrong — I would not admit I am wrong. But we are very different people, and the difference in our make-up is likely to make him champion jockey. The current state of play is that Pete has ridden 62 winners, Simon 53 and I am on 51 after an easy success on Juven Light at Lingfield today.

SUNDAY 16 MARCH
The thing I most needed after the past week was a quiet, slovenly day in an armchair ... and that is exactly what I had today. With no snooker partner and the passing of the American football season, both my usual Sunday pursuits are off the menu so I became a goggle-eyed telly addict for the afternoon and evening, simply trying to recharge somewhat over-used batteries.

MONDAY 17 MARCH
My guv'nor Nicky flew to Ireland today with an urgent mission. The Italian owners of See You Then have been on to him with a request that their horse should pass up his engagement at the Aintree National meeting and instead try for a rich hurdle race in Italy. You can't blame them for wanting to show off their champion in their homeland, but Nicky is anxious to run the horse at Liverpool. As a compromise, he has agreed to try and buy these fellows another horse to run in Italy. Watch this space for developments.

I set off on the previously arduous journey from Newmarket to Plumpton and was mildly amazed to get there in one-and-a-half hours. The M25, now open almost all the way round London, is beginning to pamper us racing gypsies. Before they built it, this journey was a three-hour nightmare, and I hate to think how long it used to take before there were any motorways at all. It was a worthwhile trip, too — Foyle Fisherman won again, restoring a contact with John Jenkins I seemed to have lost over recent weeks.

TUESDAY 18 MARCH
In two days' time flat racing begins again up at Doncaster. The only difference this makes to my way of life for the next couple of months is that jumping receives substantially less of the racing publicity than has been the case up to now. Otherwise, life goes

on as before. But here in Newmarket, headquarters of the summer game, I can feel the atmosphere building up to a crescendo.

The town sleeps during the winter, while I am chasing busily around the country. Now it is as if an electric charge has been passed through the place — everyone is buzzing and bubbling, and when I ride out on the Heath at dawn there is the animated sight of up to 2,000 horses queuing to use the gallops, trainers and their staff bustling about with furrowed brows, and touts with their high-powered glasses and notebooks clocking the action. I have very little time to follow the flat myself, except on the odd occasion when jumpers I have ridden turn out in distance events, but when living in Newmarket it is impossible — and undesirable! — to avoid being drawn into the social scene.

The post-Cheltenham jumping today could also aptly have been described as flat, my one ride at Nottingham resulting in the worst of all results, unseated from the favourite in a novice hurdle. It was made worse by the fact that the horse, Gavin's Bell Founder, was absolutely running away and would undoubtedly have won if I had remained on board. The only consolation was that I picked myself up unscathed. Only my pride was hurt on a day when Simon Sherwood injured his neck, a hospital case which will cost him a week's rides, and there were nasty-looking falls for Peter 'Scu' and Graham Bradley. So perhaps I should be counting my blessings.

WEDNESDAY 19 MARCH
Many jockeys are superstitious. As a general rule, I am not, but I am considering the point very carefully tonight. Yesterday morning I bought a new pair of shoes — red sneakers to wear with jeans at the meetings where it is not necessary to dress up. I wore them to Nottingham yesterday, when I was unseated, and I wore them again to Worcester today, where I was obliged to pull up on every one of my four rides. So since I mistakenly purchased these sneakers, I have failed to complete in any one of five races.

THURSDAY 20 MARCH
Reading this morning's *Sporting Life* I was astonished to see the

name of P. Scudamore chalked up against a particularly dodgy jumper in the novice chase at Towcester. I wondered what on earth Pete was thinking of, taking a ride like that at this delicate stage of the season, midway between Cheltenham and Liverpool and with the jockeys' title still at stake. So, when I got to the course, I sought him out and told him so. In fact I gave him a bit of a bollocking for being stupid and, to his credit, he took the point and did get out of the ride.

Sure enough, the horse buried the deputy pilot Allen Webb at one of the uphill fences, leaving him motionless for several minutes. That could have been the end of 'Scu's' season and the end of his bid for the championship. He came up later and thanked me, but he really shouldn't accept rides like that in the first place. No one thinks any the better of you for it. I know, as I have previously said, that the reason he will probably be champion ahead of me is that he is prepared to chase rides rather more than I do, but there must come a time when you touch the brake and hold back for the sake of expediency and good health.

FRIDAY 21 MARCH

There was decent racing at Newbury, but no luck for me, although there was hope for the future from two runners-up. Whitsunday, a chaser having his first run under rules after three point-to-point wins by no less than 25 lengths, shaped very impressively before being run out of it from the last, and I was very unlucky on another horse of Nicky's, the novice hurdler Arnhall. We knew that he hates being in front, and it was my plan to hold him up behind the leaders until the last possible moment, as he has plenty of finishing speed. This was thwarted by complete accident. At the second last flight I was nicely tucked in behind the pacemaker, ridden by Phil Tuck, when he fell and broke a leg. This left me a very reluctant leader, and I had no alternative but to go for home. Just as I had feared, Arnhall folded up after the last and was beaten one-and-a-half lengths into second place.

In both races I had been beaten by horses trained by Captain Tim Forster and ridden by Hywel Davies. It was a welcome change of luck for them both. The poor Captain had lost no fewer than three of his better horses this week, all killed in various ways, and must have been in the depths of despair, while Hywel, who takes the job every bit as seriously as his pal 'Scu', had been very short of winners and getting extremely low about it. Amazingly, they went on to register a four-timer, which must be one of the greatest swings of the fortune pendulum this season has seen. I'm pleased for them both.

SATURDAY 22 MARCH

I stayed at the Francomes last night, and heard another of John's ambitious schemes for his life. Training is not turning out quite as well as he had hoped yet, and he tells me he is tempted to take a year off and spend it travelling around the world. He wants me to go with him. Now, there are times when I get depressed about my lot and there is nothing I would rather do than pull up stumps on the jockey's life and set off to explore the world, but it only takes a few minutes to convince me it is a fantasy I could never live out. Being a Gemini, I am a Jekyll and Hyde character and it is only in one of my guises that these ideas even enter my head; fortunately, I always return to my more familiar role in time to realise that I have too many responsibilities, too many commitments both to myself and to those close to me, to ever carry through something so outrageous. Basically, I come from a very solid family background and I have pretty settled, domesticated views of life. John, however is the type who might just carry out the threat. I only hope he realises that to do that would probably ruin his training career for good. It is hard enough to set up a training establishment once and get the trust of sufficient owners. To do it twice is asking too much.

Besides, I won a big race today, so all is right with my world! Pikes Peak duly justified favouritism in the Philip Cornes Hurdle final at Newbury and is proving to be one of the stars of the season, unlike John Jenkins' Ivy League, who flopped yet again and is now looking a very expensive piece of dogmeat.

SUNDAY 23 MARCH

Tom Jones taught me most of what I know about horses and racing when I worked for him as an apprentice. I respected him enormously and still do, so the relationship continues very much in the style of master and servant, trainer and apprentice, despite the fact that I now live with his daughter. There are occasions, however, when the barriers are broken down — usually when we get drunk together after a family get-together. We had just such a party today, lunch blending into supper and Sunday becoming Monday almost before I knew it, and it is amazing how a decanter of port can stimulate good debate!

MONDAY 24 MARCH

A car service, haircut and paperwork were all I had in the diary today. But I wasn't sorry not to be riding. The spring winds outside whipped up to such a temper that they knocked down my chicken shed and a fence, and left one of my plum trees leaning drunkenly. It would not have been much fun riding a novice chaser around Wolverhampton in this.

TUESDAY 25 MARCH

Sandown ran a very strange card today, which included two races for amateur riders and one for conditional jockeys, leaving three open to the professionals. With the fields small, I didn't get a single ride, which at least left me clear to repair the storm damage in my garden, even if it wasn't very welcome in most ways.

Pete Scudamore is still going very well and has now extended his lead to ten in the jockeys' table. More than two months of the season still remain, but in my heart I have accepted that I am most unlikely to finish as champion. I had a very good chance when the season began — indeed, I may never have a better one — but winners are hard to come by at this end of the campaign and, as I have said, I am not prepared to risk my neck riding anything outlandish. If 'Scu' was injured tomorrow, and ruled out of the remainder of the season, I would have to sit down and give serious thought to trying to catch him, but if he stays fit I shall still be content with what I have achieved this year.

WEDNESDAY 26 MARCH

The Italian Job has resolved itself. Nicky bought a horse called Duplicator, a top Irish four-year-old trained by Mick O'Toole, and that will be sent over for the race in Italy over Easter. I, by coincidence, will be heading the opposite way to Ireland, having been offered the ride on Run and Skip in the Irish Grand National at Fairyhouse.

THURSDAY 27 MARCH

Racing was at Ludlow and Southwell, and my only offered ride was a novice hurdler for Nick in a race at the Shropshire track. Now, Newmarket to Ludlow is a pig of a journey at the best of times, and today I felt very disinclined to attempt it for the sake of one little horse without a hope in hell of winning. Fortunately, the owner saw things the same way — he didn't want to go either, so Nicky took the horse out and everyone was happy.

I filled in the time organising my trip to Ireland and assuaging my slight pangs of guilt over not staying at home to scratch around for half-a-dozen rides at one of the Bank Holiday meetings here. Maybe I should be doing that. Call it complacency if you like, but I know I would probably have taken the opposite decision if I still felt I had any chance in the championship. So, bearing in mind my predilection for the social habits of the Irish, I will fly out to Dublin on Saturday night and make a decent weekend of it, with the lure of a tilt at the big race to top it off on Monday.

FRIDAY 28 MARCH

When I listed 'bird-watching' among my hobbies in the *Turf Guide* (the bible of racing folk) I did not have my tongue in cheek — I really did mean the feathered variety. Plenty of people are willing to believe that the only birds I study are two-legged, but in fact I have made myself pretty knowledgeable on ornithology and I love visiting bird sanctuaries to look at unfamiliar species. Today I drove to the Norfolk coast with just that in mind. I have a lot to think about at the moment, and when I have things to contemplate and decisions to take I very often head for the beach and a solitary stroll. With the sea breeze blowing the cobwebs out of my brain I could think clearly, and an afternoon visit to the sanctuary completed an enjoyably worthwhile day, far from the crowds I often crave but sometimes loathe.

SATURDAY 29 MARCH

Races cut up badly over the Easter holiday, and this year is no exception. It annually gives owners and trainers their best chance of winning a little event with a poor animal, and it always draws big crowds into the courses, so it should not be knocked, but there was some very modest fare at Towcester today. I did manage to ride a winner on Nicky's novice chaser Edenspring, however, before hurrying on to catch the 8.00 p.m. flight out of Heathrow with a friend named Mick Curtain. We booked into Jury's Hotel in Dublin and had a relatively early night; it is likely to be the only one during our stay.

SUNDAY 30 MARCH

A trip to Ireland really is like going home for me. I have a lot of affinity with their way of life here, and I just love their sense of humour. Today we met up with some of the Irish jockeys, notably Tommy McGivern, and needless to say it was a day of riotous sociability.

MONDAY 31 MARCH

Run and Skip had been allotted top weight of 12 stone in the National. He was also just 'over the top' after so many brave efforts in tough company this season, and it was bottomless mud at Fairyhouse this afternoon after 24 hours of solid heavy rain. A combination of these three factors made certain that the Irish National did not join my list of big races won.

Conditions were dire by English standards — the Irish relish the boggy ground rather more than we do — and although my horse ran his heart out yet again, the writing was on the wall a long way from home. I was still in fourth place as we jumped the third last, but with no chance of winning. I was wondering whether to pull up or not when a panting and snorting alongside announced the arrival of my good Yorkshire pal Graham Bradley, riding Righthand Man for Mrs Dickinson. His horse was in the same state as mine — thoroughly knackered — and in his broadest, most breathless tones he muttered: 'Eee, ah wish ah could pull up'. Seeing the chance of ending the agony in a bit of fun, I replied: 'Just follow me', and turned sharply left-handed, steering him off the course. The expression on Brad's face was a picture — horror and shock with just a degree of relief — but we were soon laughing about it on the muddy, wet walk back to the weighing-room. Significantly, the first three places in the race were all occupied by horses carrying less than ten stone. It was not a day for class weight-carrying animals; the moderate sloggers won out.

In the bar I bumped into 'Ginger' McCain, who I expect to be seeing rather a lot this week, as I shall be staying very close to his Southport stables for the National meeting. This initiated a farewell session on the whisky, which progressed to a local pub which boasted, among its decorations, a stuffed pheasant. Or rather, it used to. That stuffed pheasant, now mysteriously headless, somehow ended the night inside my pocket. It will be something to surprise the boys with later in the week....

Back in London, I checked the day's results and found I had not missed a single winner by opting for Ireland. But Simon Sherwood rode four winners at Newton Abbot. Perhaps I will struggle for second place in the table, now.

APRIL

THURSDAY 3 APRIL

I don't always look forward to Liverpool, but this year has been different. With an enviable National ride in Classified, and three likely winners in River Ceiriog, See You Then and Kathies Lad, I would not willingly have swapped places with any other jockey as we drove north up the M6 this morning. By tonight, I was not so sure. What a difference a day can make!

Di usually comes up with me for this three-day meeting and, this year, we had decided to stay in Southport, at the busy but remote Royal Clifton, rather than risking the Irish contingent, who set up base at Liverpool's Holiday Inn. In my younger days, I would have been with them, but there are important horses to be ridden this year — and, anyway, I reasoned, an awful lot of racing people stay in Southport and it is certain to be just as much fun.

The first thing to go awry was not long in coming. Just as at Cheltenham, the opening event of Liverpool's three-day meeting is a valuable two-mile novice hurdle. River Ceiriog had trounced most of this opposition three weeks before, and I saw no good reason why he should not do so again, despite having to give weight away all round. I had carefully scrutinised the form of every horse in the race and, although there were dangers, I set off to the start as confident as any jockey has the right to be.

Three hurdles from home I was cruising. I had held the horse up longer than at Cheltenham, trusting in his finishing kick, and as I went past half the field on the bridle I felt my confidence had been entirely justified. Two out, I was disputing the lead and I thought it only a matter of time before I saw off all challengers. But as we approached the last the alarm bells began to ring in my

136

head. One horse, his jockey clad in the distinctive blue-and-white hoops of Terry Ramsden, was still with me and showing no sign of throwing in the towel. I went for everything. River Ceiriog hit the final flight, but I am not sure it made the slightest difference to the outcome. All the way up the run-in I was coming off second-best and, at the line, the margin was three-quarters of a length.

I have to say I had given I Bin Zaidoon no chance, which I suppose is always dangerous with a horse of Mr Ramsden's. The man himself was waiting to welcome his winner, surrounded by what seemed like a dozen minders. He is certainly a colourful character, probably good for the game, and on most other occasions I would have enjoyed the scene, but not today. I had been so sure that River Ceiriog would win, and this came as a savage setback. With hindsight, it doesn't seem so bad. Things seldom do. He was, after all, giving the winner pounds, which means that strictly on the book he was still the best horse in the race. I don't think the tight Aintree circuit suited him and nor, looking back, do I think I rode him to his best advantage. He is a relentless galloper, suited by being up at the head of affairs, and maybe he was held up too long.

But the fact remains I was bitterly disappointed, a feeling which was not assuaged when Indamelody, another horse I had fancied — if more quietly — ran well enough but could finish only third in the stayers' handicap hurdle. The meeting seemed to be crumbling beneath my feet. And so, not having any further rides, and having met up with some of the Irish jockeys I had been with in Dublin only a few days ago, I decided to have a few drinks and try to put the dejection out of sight and out of mind . . . .

FRIDAY 4 APRIL

Thursday ran inconveniently into Friday, and I have an awful feeling I have made a fool of myself in the most spectacular fashion. In brief, since my last ride on Thursday, I have got drunk, had a fearful row with Di, been hijacked in my own car and then stupidly confessed the lot on television. The first three circumstances are temporarily painful but no more; the last may have altogether more serious ramifications.

To explain myself I need to go back to early yesterday evening. I drove back to Southport with Di to check into the hotel, still feeling sorry for myself. The Irish boys, most of whom were over for a busman's holiday, had bought me a scotch or two and cheered me up with their wit, but I was still sober and still depressed. So I took it out on Di. It was unfair, of course, but it happened. I told her I was going out for the evening in Liverpool and, to put it mildly, we had a ruck. It was made fairly plain that I had better find somewhere else to sleep and, the lady not being short of character, I knew she meant it.

I left the hotel, now angry as well as depressed. But when I got into my car I couldn't face the long drive back into the city, so instead I just drove around the corner to a place where I knew there would be a welcome — Ginger and Beryl McCain's house. I find the McCains great company, and I was soon beginning to forget my problems, helped by liberal quantities of scotch and some excellent food. I left them at a respectable hour, certainly before midnight, and faced up to my dilemma again. It didn't even occur to me to try and find another hotel room — I knew the two major hotels in Southport were full and I was in no state to go farther afield, so I decided to spend the night in the back of my car. It was no big deal — I have used it before as a last resort, and being a Mercedes it is not uncomfortable. The problem was, I was by now quite drunk, and as I stumbled back into the car I must have left the keys either in the doorlock or in the ignition — I honestly can't remember which. Oblivious to this, I covered myself up with a couple of overcoats against what was a distinctly chilly night, and then settled down to sleep.

The next thing I was aware of was a strange sensation of movement. It can only have been an hour or two later, and I was in that indefinable limbo somewhere between sleep and wakefulness. I tried to concentrate my befuddled brain, and there really was no doubt. Then it hit me — where I was, what I was doing there and the dramatic realisation that, if I wasn't driving the car, someone else had to be. I burst out from under my covering of coats, sat up sharply in the back seat and said something abrupt and absurd: 'What the hell do you think you're doing?'

The driver, I now saw, was a teenage bloke, a joyrider no

doubt, and the effect on him of my sudden words and actions was, I imagine, not unlike that on someone convinced he has seen a ghost. He gave a terrified squeak, slammed on the brakes, swerved the car rapidly and awkwardly onto the hard shoulder and, without pausing for polite conversation, opened the door and legged it. He was halfway across a field which bordered the road before I had fully realised what he was doing, and then there seemed no point in chasing him. I surveyed the scene and counted my problems. Thanks to an obliging traffic sign I was able to ascertain that I was on the M57, approximately 20 miles from Southport, so that was one potential teaser solved. But I still had to get myself back to the hotel, and I was well aware I would not have passed a breathaliser. Still, there was no option; I could hardly just sit there, on the hard shoulder of the motorway, waiting for an inevitable police patrol car to come along. So I got back into the driver's seat and, feeling slightly shaky for the experience and no doubt a little hazy for the alcohol, I navigated back to Southport surprisingly accurately, re-parked in the hotel car park, locked all the doors and dozed off again — this time in the driver's seat and with the engine left on to heat the car.

When at last I woke again in daylight and reconstructed the events, it seemed scarcely believable. I was stone-cold sober now, and ready to admit that it might also have been frightening. But, after all, it had turned out all right, hadn't it — and it was a great yarn to tell the lads in the weighing-room. So I set off for the races, if not exactly with a song in my heart then certainly feeling much bouncier than I had been yesterday evening.

To be honest, I was bursting to tell someone the story, and as the first person I saw was my valet Johnny Buckingham, he was regaled with the entire saga. Knowing me as well as he does, he didn't disbelieve it, either — indeed, he was so struck by it that he, naturally enough, relayed it to a few other willing listeners. By this time I had also retold the story once or twice, and before I knew what was happening everyone on the course seemed to have heard it in some form or other and I was being asked to go on television for a chat with their usual interviewer Jonathan Powell. I saw nothing wrong with the idea and answered Jonathan's questions faithfully, glossing over the row with Di, but otherwise being brutally honest right down to confessing that the reason I had not chased my kidnapper was that I was thoroughly drunk.

Tonight, just a few hours on, I realise this admission was stupid, quite probably one of the silliest things I have ever said, and I am fully expecting trouble over it. Not from the police — I have not reported the matter and there is nothing they could now do about it — but perhaps from Nicky and his owners, if they should take the view that it was careless at best and irresponsible at worst first to get drunk and then blunder into a situation as potentially dangerous as that, during one of the season's most important meetings. Nicky thought the whole thing very amusing when he first heard of it but, like me, he has now had time to appraise the question not of what did happen but what might have happened. What if there had been two blokes instead of just one? What if the joyrider had been armed, maybe with a knife? And what if he had crashed the car? All these possible consequences have now occurred to me, and I must say the affair does not seem quite so funny any more.

The conspiracy of circumstances which led me into the trap could, I suppose, all have been avoided, though it really stemmed from the bitter disappointment which beset me following River Ceiriog's defeat. Oddly enough, that horse is owned by Mr Bobby McAlpine, who also owns Baby Sigh, the only horse I had to ride today. He had absolutely no chance in one of the best four-year-old races of the season, but I put him in the race and did my best on him. He finished tailed off, just as I imagined he would.

There was no way I was going to involve myself in another drinking session tonight, and as I have not yet patched up my differences with Di, I checked into another, smaller hotel in Southport, where the Francomes are staying. I was in thoughtful mood and determined to keep a low profile, so after an early dinner I retired to bed at 10.30 p.m., anxious to catch up on some sleep in the knowledge that my riding tomorrow might be scrutinised that bit more critically than usual.

SATURDAY 5 APRIL

My usual papers, the *Daily Express* and *Sporting Life*, were waiting for me on the table when I went in to breakfast. Normally, I would have picked up the *Life* first — especially on National morning — but my eye was drawn irresistibly to the front page of the *Express*, and it gave me quite a turn. Splash headline, dramatic words and a picture, too — my kidnap saga, leading the front page. I suppose I should have seen it coming, but it had honestly never occurred to me that the papers would give the story such treatment.

I glanced sheepishly around the room and noticed a good deal of whispering and nudging going on. That told me all I needed to know. The story was obviously in their papers, too. I didn't much enjoy my breakfast. It's all very well being a celebrity, but I could predict all too clearly the frosty reaction such notoriety might bring from one or two owners I ride for, and I couldn't really blame them.

As ever on National day I left very early to beat the traffic queues outside the course. I was prepared for the ribbing in the weighing-room, which was all good-natured, but I was taken aback by my reception when I went out for my ride on Kathies Lad in the day's first race. There was a fantastic crowd at Aintree, probably the biggest I have ever seen there, and I don't suppose there were many in the mass who had not read about my adventures in their morning papers. As I walked Kathies Lad out of the parade ring, the jibes were many and audible.

'Do you need a chauffeur, Steve?'

'Had your car pinched lately, Smith Eccles?' . . . And other, less polite enquiries. It was, I admit, a little unnerving. I had already detected that a proportion of people didn't believe the story at all, while others were convinced that there was rather more to it than I had made out. The fact that there wasn't didn't help me. I knew I had already said far too much about the business and that now I had to ride at my very best and strongest to avoid any possibility of the muttering becoming plain indignation. I have never let my social life affect my riding, but I knew that plea was going to sound pathetic if I failed to do myself justice now.

Well, I am proud of the ride I turned in on Kathies Lad. In the season's richest two-miles handicap chase, he won for the second successive year and, it transpired, did so despite considerable pain from a plate which twisted into his hoof during the race. It must have been that which made him jump violently left at the last, but although many spectators expected a stewards' enquiry, I always felt I was clear of the chasing horses and had hampered nobody. Brave horse that he is, Kathies then sprinted away on the run-in to win by two-and-a-half lengths and I came back feeling considerably relieved.

That, I thought, was the hard bit done. I expected See You Then to win the Sandeman Aintree Hurdle, and I expected that I would be required to do little more than steer. But, not for the first time this week, I was wrong. He had never attempted two miles five furlongs before, but he had won a slow-run race at Doncaster over only a furlong less, so, before the event, we were not unduly concerned about his ability to get the trip. He had previously trounced every horse in the field, so we were justified in thinking he should win and the betting market, which had him at 9-4 on, supported our conviction.

The horse did not help his chances by pulling hard early on. I had a battle to settle him, but once he stopped fighting me he was travelling smoothly. Turning out of the back straight, Aonoch made his move under Jimmy Duggan. I had expected that and I went with him, tracking him into the straight, always going well. See You Then got close to the second last, losing momentum, but now it was clear that I had a struggle on hand. The ground was sticky after morning rain and I wondered, aghast, if my horse could produce his devastating finishing speed.

Coming to the last I had to press the button, ask the horse questions he had never needed to answer at Cheltenham. For a time, it seemed he would respond like a true champion. I got the rail and drove him up the inside of Aonoch, who was staying on gallantly. I was within a neck of him 100 yards from the line, but even as I got there, I had the horrible sensation of running out of petrol. See You Then simply had no more to give, and was beaten by a length. We had taken him to Liverpool for easy pickings and come unstuck. I don't think he liked either the track or the trip. He is a top-class two-miler and I suspect he will be kept to that from now on.

Nicky did not condemn me at all, but I still felt low. In the minutes which followed I rode the race time and again in my head, and I know there is nothing more I could have done to win. It was, however, another nasty pill to swallow, and at a most unfortunate time.

I had to get myself motivated again for the National. I sat sipping tea in my corner of the weighing-room, while all around me the excited chatter which traditionally precedes the greatest spectacle of the jumping season ebbed and flowed. The youngsters, those for whom it was all new, were the most animated, but some old heads, too, were bubbling. It seemed to me, as I sat a little detached from the hubbub, that everyone was asking everyone else how they would run and nobody was listening to the obviously optimistic answers. And then came the ritual in which National jockeys always get all their colleagues to sign the race-card over the name of their ride. It is a harmless souvenir, but I was in no mood to join in, and after signing several I was a bit short when the teaboys came round asking me for my autograph.

The reason why the National meant nothing special to me is that, in my previous six attempts, I had only managed to complete the course once. I had twice finished up fishing in Bechers Brook and I had never looked like winning the race, so history did not exactly fill me with confidence or enthusiasm. Having said that, I considered Classified to be one of the best National rides I had ever had. He is not a big, robust horse but he is an athlete, a natural, safe jumper, best at two or two-and-a-half miles on park courses but not short on stamina, as he showed when completing in fifth place last year. This season he had been trained specifically with the National in mind, and he was spot-on for the occasion. I cheered myself up with the thought that he might even improve my dismal Aintree record.

In many diverse ways, the National is unique. One striking thing about it is the noise which assails the jockeys' ears as the tapes go up and the field surges away from the packed stands. In any normal race you are oblivious to the crowd, but here the roar is deafening. There is another audible cheer from the crowd out at Bechers, for those who get that far. This year, as usual, there were plenty who failed. I had jumped off towards the outer, ignoring the usual scrum for the rail, because the first six fences are in a straight line and there is plenty of opportunity to track over to the inner once your horse is settled. I broke fast and first out of the gate, always doubly important in this enormous field of 40, and as we went to the first I noticed Graham McCourt, on Tim Forster's Port Askaig, ranging upsides.

I called across: 'This is it then, here we go'.

He shouted back: 'I'll just be glad to get over this first fence'.

The first always catches out a few horses. It is the steepness of the drop which is the surprise element, and although Classified — suitably steadied a few yards before take-off — met it perfectly, I still landed with a jolt. Even as I did so I heard the tell-tale tinkling of irons from my right which always signifies a faller. Poor Graham had hit the deck and Richard Rowe, on the third favourite Door Latch, had come to grief with him. Back in the weighing-room much later a laconic Rowe was heard to report that it was such a pity because he had been going so well at the time!

The third fence is the first big ditch. It sorts out the men from the boys, and Classified was foot-perfect. Once over that, I had a feeling of rising confidence. Barring accidents, I knew I was in for a decent ride, and I actually began to enjoy myself.

Essex, the Czech entry, was weaving all over the course, and I was fully occupied avoiding him for a while, but by Bechers I was in the clear again. Jumping this extraordinary brook is like going into space, but Classified was brave and accurate. We landed running and I decided that the time was right to tack over to the inside. By the time we crossed the Melling Road, only West Tip and Richard Dunwoody were on my inner and I was perfectly satisfied with my position.

Over the awesome Chair and past the stands again, lying about sixth, a loose horse began to worry me. He was jumping the fences, edging right at each one, so I made sure I stayed on his inside. Sure enough, at the 17th he went quite violently right, bringing down one runner and badly interfering with another. That, then, was another danger met and matched.

At the 22nd — Bechers for the second time — I took the lead. I didn't really want to be there, but Classified had jumped to the front and was plainly enjoying it all, so there was absolutely no point in restraining him. By now, too, I had changed my thinking about the Grand National — thanks to Classified. I defy anyone to find a thrill comparable with jumping these Aintree fences on a thoroughly good horse. I can't describe it, and I can only imagine it must be like being high on drugs, only without the side effects.

I knew, however, that there was only a certain amount of fuel left in Classified's tank, and when Chris Grant on Young Driver ranged alongside at the third last, I felt pretty sure we were not going to win. I was also well aware that West Tip was creeping ever closer up the rail.

'Rambo' Grant — if you saw his spindly body you would appreciate the nickname — is a great character of the northern courses, but all the same I tried a bit of psychology, calling across to him to go steady as we still had a long way to go. It didn't work — his response was to wave his whip and kick for home, leaving me trailing.

I badly wanted to complete, but while there was still a chance I had to ask Classified for one final effort. To his eternal credit, he responsed, albeit at one tired pace. It is in these final yards that the National can be a cruel race. A horse may have relished the jumping but now, when he has nothing left to give, his jockey is still obliged to demand more. In any other race I would have pulled him up but we plugged on, while up ahead West Tip remorselessly gunned down Young Driver on the run-in through a coolly inspired piece of riding. Richard was fantastic, and as I saw him go past the winning post from 20 lengths further back I was delighted for him. I was also delighted for myself. Third place in the National may not earn much of the glamour, but it earns the owner a good payout, and it gave me an experience I shall never forget. Nicky was ecstatic, too ... and nobody, surely, could say my riding had in any way suffered through my well-publicised social activities.

If the weighing-room is noisy before the National, it is nothing to the uproar immediately afterwards, as all the boys talk each other through the race fence by fence, reliving every slice of the action. By now, I even felt up to joining in, although I was shattered by the effort I had expended. It is always an anti-climax to have to go out and ride in the last race on the card, the only other one open to professionals, and this year it was worse than ever. Most of the crowd had gone and an ordinary novice hurdle seemed somehow irrelevant. My horse, Bell Founder, ran a stinker and, all things considered, I think I may try to avoid taking a ride in the race next year.

I was too tired to drive back to Newmarket, so I went back to my small Southport hotel and wound down with another evening at Ginger McCains. It has been an emotional, memorable day in many ways but at the end of it I fear the Aintree chapter is not yet closed.

SUNDAY 6 APRIL

I phoned my parents, and was not surprised to hear that they were upset by the publicity I had received. The local Derbyshire press had also been in touch with them over the story, which struck me as unnecessary and possibly malicious, and my mother was ready with a few stern words of advice for me. I didn't have to do any explaining, she had already worked out the truth of the story, and as usual her advice was sound.

I drove home and, not without difficulty, patched things up with Di. It is silly to think that all this stemmed from an over-reaction to one defeat, but that is the case. I know now I was foolishly stubborn, and that the mess I got myself into on Thursday night was self-induced. It was also unprofessional, and I am not proud of that. We all make mistakes, but just at the moment I seem to be making more than my share.

WEDNESDAY 9 APRIL

Ascot: one of the last major meetings of the season. There are still plenty of whispers around about my Liverpool escapade, but I try hard not to discuss it now — I want to put it behind me. I thought I would ride a winner today on Juven Light, but he ran unaccountably badly, as did my other mount, Joy Ride. Poor Jeff King is having a wretched time, and there was no spark at all in the horse. It can happen to any trainer, and it is not always possible to pinpoint a reason. I just hope things come right for Kingy, because I like him a lot.

There is talk today of Peter Scudamore being offered the job as stable jockey to Fred Winter next season. It might be difficult for him, after spending so long under the wing of David Nicholson, but I think he would be silly to turn it down.

THURSDAY 10 APRIL

I had arranged to go to Southwell to ride two of Nicky's hurdlers, so I took a spare ride offered. Then Nicky took his two horses out, and I was obliged to make the journey for one no-hoper. At this late stage of the season, such is life. I have now slipped to fourth place in the table, behind Hywel Davies, so I need to get my finger out.

FRIDAY 11 APRIL

As the Saturday meeting is again at Ascot I had arranged to stay the night with Nicky Henderson in Lambourn. I knew what I was letting myself in for and I went prepared for an inquest into the happenings of a week ago. Fortified by riding a winner for Jeff King at Towcester, I arrived at Windsor House at the cocktail hour, accompanied by Di, and Nick and I went into conclave to talk things through.

I made no attempt to offer excuses or cover anything up. There was tension in the air and I knew Nick had taken some flak from certain owners, so for his sake as well as mine I simply made a clean breast of it, told him I had done wrong and that I would not do anything so unprofessional again. It was a frank talk, and very worthwhile for both of us. I still want to ride for Nick next season and I am pretty sure he wants me around, so clearing the air today was essential.

SATURDAY 12 APRIL

I thought I had had a stroke of luck this morning when Fred Winter approached me on the Lambourn gallops and asked me to ride his novice chaser Gold Bearer at Ascot this afternoon. It turned out, however, to be a case of being in the right place at the wrong time, because Gold Bearer dumped me on the deck at the third fence. In fact, Fred's first three runners of the meeting, all fancied, ended on the floor, so it was as well that Lambourn pride was retrieved by Nick's very promising chaser Whitsunday, who jumped splendidly and made all the running to give me my 57th winner and give Nick a dilemma. The ground is sure to dry up soon, discouraging him from running his better horses, but as this was the horse's first win under rules, he will be anxious to win another with him before he has to turn to handicapping next season. I'm glad it's not my problem.

Nick had a valuable double, as Pikes Peak graduated to handicap company and slaughtered the opposition. But this was a ride I was frustrated in missing. Nick decided to put the stable claimer Michael Bowlby on him to take off seven pounds and, as he won, the move was justified. It's not a precedent which delights me, however.

'Scu' has decided to join Fred Winter next season, and announced it to the press before racing. David Nicholson was then interviewed on TV and gave me the distinct impression that it was not the best news he has had this week. I hope they remain friends, but I don't think 'Scu' could have taken any other course. Fred may have had a quiet season by his own standards, but it is still one of the best jobs in racing.

MONDAY 14 APRIL
With no racing today, and rides booked at Devon tomorrow, the temptation was too great — I drove down to Torquay this afternoon with 'Sharky' Sherwood and booked into the Palace Hotel. It was the first time I had stayed there for months but the welcome was as overwhelming as ever, from the manager Paul Uphill — who found rooms for us both despite the fact that they were officially full up — down to Jeff the barman, Vic in the restaurant and David the head porter. I think if I could use the Palace as my HQ for the entire racing season I would not hesitate to do so.

TUESDAY 15 APRIL
In torrential rain there is no worse racecourse to be stranded on than Haldon in Devon. Set on the side of a hill, open to all the elements, it attracts the very worst of bad weather and then revels in it. It is a long, galloping course, and when you are at the

farthest point from the stands on a grim, wet and windy day like today you might just as well be on horseback in the middle of Dartmoor. It was so wet, indeed, that racing was put back half-an-hour, and conditions were barely tolerable when we did start. I thought it was going to be one of those days when Kathies Lad, widely regarded as a good thing for the feature event, showed very little interest and was beaten after jumping three fences. I fear he is over the top and has simply had enough for the season. But my day was redeemed when Bluelimit won the handicap hurdle. It was a chance ride for me, the horse being trained by David Elsworth, and I know the owners had a nice touch on him.

A final thought today for the unsung heroes of muddy meetings, the valets. Racegoers never see them, these tireless backroom workers, but you can take it from me that they earn their money at all times, never more so than when the weather is as it was today and their job becomes a thankless slog. John Buckingham, who looks after me, has already been mentioned, but there are a dozen or more like him up and down the country. Those on duty at Devon today would have still been in the weighing-room three hours after the last race, probably covered in mud. It's not a job I can ever see myself doing, but I'm very thankful they are around.

WEDNESDAY 16 APRIL

Jonjo's falls really are becoming inconvenient. At Cheltenham today we were going round together in the three-mile handicap hurdle, both on horses with little chance. I was telling him a particularly funny joke and was just about to deliver the punch-line when he came down! He got a pretty severe kicking, but he couldn't wait to get back into the weighing-room and hear the end of the joke.

THURSDAY 17 APRIL

If ever I have a daydream about going into films when I give up riding, I shall remember today and dismiss the idea immediately. John Francome and I had been asked to make a video advertising a Timeshare company with whom we have linked up. It was

149

hardly a taxing part for us — we had just the one line to introduce ourselves, and we had to say it together. But every time we began, we would catch sight of each other's anxiously concentrating expressions and burst out laughing. We did get through it eventually . . . on take 51.

FRIDAY 18 APRIL

I have won a big race; I have been spoiled to pieces and I feel as if, just for once, I have sampled the jet-set world in which the leading flat jockeys exist. I have to say I could get a taste for it!

It was Scottish Champion Hurdle day at Ayr, and Nicky had entered River Ceiriog for what will undoubtedly be his final race of the season. Now, the drive up to Scotland would not have been an appealing prospect but, thankfully, we were spared the ordeal and instead, travelled in considerable style. Nick's wife Diana drove us from Lambourn to Wolverhampton where we boarded Bobby McAlpine's private executive plane, stopping off at Chester to pick up the owner himself, and then flying on to land near the Ayr course.

I had always maintained that River Ceiriog was the best two-mile novice in the country, even after his defeat at Liverpool and, although he was today taking on the second, third and fourth horses home in the Champion at Cheltenham, he was getting weight from them all and I gave him a decent chance. We decided that he should make his own running if necessary, as he is a much better horse with a strong gallop, and the plan worked to perfection. Nothing else so much as got in a blow at him, and he was a very convincing winner, fully redeeming himself for the Aintree disappointment.

That put me in a high good humour, maintained by the natural wit of my northern jockey pals — especially Colin 'Jack' Hawkins, a night bird when he gets the chance, and today sporting a fierce black eye from some mysterious fracas on the streets of Ayr last evening.

A perfect day ended in another painless plane journey. We were back in Lambourn almost before we knew it, and in plenty of time for a celebratory glass.

SATURDAY 19 APRIL

Schooled Indamelody over fences again. He is potentially a very useful chaser but he has no confidence to go for the long ones; if he is to get round safely he just has to get in close to the obstacles and pop over, which is frustrating for a jockey and rather self-defeating within a race. It is engrained in every decent jockey to look for the stride approaching each fence and, if it is right, to commit the horse to the long take-off. With a horse of Indamelody's disposition, that isn't possible, but it is very hard to change the basically good habits built up over the years. The horse is scheduled to go to Nottingham for a novice chase next Tuesday, which should be interesting.

I had thought this was going to be a very ordinary day at the office, with just a couple of rides at Stratford, but it turned out quite well, as I got Welsh Oak up to win the handicap hurdle for David Gandolfo.

SUNDAY 20 APRIL

There is little to report, except for a big lunch, long afternoon kip, and a lazy evening. I am badly missing my snooker partner Tommy, and so far I have not found a suitable substitute.

MONDAY 21 APRIL

The Newmarket cavaliers are breaking up fast. Simon McNeil came with me to Southwell today and, after a miserable journey in driving rain, he confided that he is moving to Lambourn at the end of the season. Soon, I might be the only jump jockey left in town.

TUESDAY 22 APRIL

Pete Shilton rang. He offered me a ticket for tomorrow night's England v Scotland game, which was good of him — but I think the main purpose of his call was to quiz me on Indamelody's chances. I told him that if I could get him round, he would definitely win, and I hope he took my advice. The horse jumped better than before, making just the one mistake, and although he looked beaten from the third last, the combination of his staying ability and my stick up his backside carried him to the front on the run-in. That puts Nicky about £35,000 ahead of his nearest rival in the winnings league, so it looks as if he will be champion trainer for the first time.

What a contrast is provided by John Jenkins, who has hit troubled times after his usual flying start to the season. I rode two for him today and they both ran like dead horses. It puzzles me that John knows they are wrong, yet keeps running them in the belief that all will come right. It's not his fault if there is a virus in his yard, but I don't think he is doing sick horses any favours by keeping them hard at work.

WEDNESDAY 23 APRIL

I don't know what has happened to our climate. This entire season, the weather has veered from one extreme to the other, always either too wet or too dry. Right now, it is unseasonably boggy, and although Worcester's meeting today surprisingly survived a morning inspection, my trainers have taken their horses out. I have plenty of potential rides left, but they are all waiting for the usual spring-time fast ground.

THURSDAY 24 APRIL

My worst fall of the season has written me off for a week ... but I consider myself fortunate to have got away so lightly. When I hit the deck, I was horribly convinced I had broken my neck again. The cause of my distress was Rhythmic Pastimes, a horse I have won on several times and one of two rides for John Jenkins which took me down to Taunton today. A few months back, Rhythmic was potentially a decent dual-purpose horse who had won his hurdle races regularly and was adapting capably to fences. I well remember him trouncing some useful opposition in a two-and-a-half mile chase at Newbury. But his jumping went to pieces soon after that, and his confidence has obviously vanished. John put him back over hurdles today, sensibly thinking that it might restore his nerve, but the remedy seems to have been applied too late. He was backing off as we went towards the first flight, then suddenly he launched himself at the hurdle, landing in its roots and taking a crashing fall, while firing me head-first into the ground.

I felt my head disappear into my shoulders and thought: 'Not again'. The ambulancemen rapidly put me in a collar and stretchered me back to the weighing-room where, although a break was ruled out, the doctor diagnosed bruising of the neck, back and legs plus concussion, and signed me off for the statutory seven days.

FRIDAY 25 APRIL

Concussion is in many ways worse than breaking a bone. Today I feel sick, dizzy and disorientated, and I know it is a feeling which will not go away for several days. It is the first time in four or five years that I have had a week's compulsory leave, and I have no clear idea what to do with it. I don't think I'll be missing much racing, although I had taken the ride on Arctic Beau for John Thorne in tomorrow's Whitbread Gold Cup at Sandown. He only has 10 stone, and if the ground dries up he has a great chance. The one consolation is that I can now eat again!

SATURDAY 26 APRIL

I watched the Whitbread on TV, and silently applauded the great ride 'Sharky' gave Plundering to win the race for Fred Winter. Arctic Beau ran a blinder to be third in ground far softer than he likes. No one will be more worried about this result than Nicky Henderson, whose old boss Fred is now just a few thousand behind him in the winnings table. It could make an interesting finale to the season. My neck and shoulders are still stiff and sore. For much of the day I have either been soaking in hot baths or applying the ultrasound machine; it has helped a bit, but I have got a blinding headache.

SUNDAY 27 APRIL

Di has taken a few days off to be with me, and we set off today on a four-day mini-holiday, kicking off with a stop at my parents' Derbyshire home. It's funny that my family appear from all quarters when they get wind that I am going to be around, and today the place with packed with aunts, uncles and cousins. But this sort of reunion happens all too seldom, and I really enjoyed it.

MONDAY 28 APRIL

Princess Anne has had her critics in the past but I won't hear a bad word said against her. I think she is a great sport — especially after tonight. We had travelled north to Beverley for a dinner-dance run in aid of Riding for the Disabled and the Injured Jockeys Fund. We had a great night on a table dominated by jockeys, and I somehow managed to manoeuvre myself into having the last waltz with the Princess. She was appreciably taller than me in her high heels, and I mumbled something to the effect. With that, she kicked off her shoes and danced barefoot!

TUESDAY 29 APRIL

A great day in the Lake District, and a riotous evening with some good friends, had a sad postscript. We had arranged to stay with Jonjo O'Neill and his wife Sheila at their lovely Cumbrian home, and tonight we went out to a marvellous restaurant on Lake Ullswater, along with Ron Barry — a recently retired character of the weighing-room — and his wife. Midway through the meal I said to Jonjo that it was great he was coming out with the British team to Australia in June. He replied that he wasn't. At first I wondered whether he had business commitments, or perhaps that Sheila was unhappy about it, but then Jonjo stunned me by saying he was going to hang up his boots. Apparently, there were complications following his latest bang on the head. Three days later he was feeling very sick and had to be admitted to hospital. Lying there in bed, dreading yet more surgery, he just arrived at the conclusion that he had reached the end of the road. A month ago, he told me of his plan to go on riding for two or three more years because he still enjoyed it. He always thought it would be terribly difficult to take the decision to stop, but now he related that, when he realised enough was enough, it was all very easy.

We will miss him like hell in the weighing-room, because I don't know of a more popular or genuine guy. To lose both 'Franc' and Jonjo in a year is a bitter blow, but at least, like John, he will be staying in the game through training.

WEDNESDAY 30 APRIL

This is the end of the most enjoyable, relaxing few days I have had in a long time. Di and I drove back home after a good lunch on Lake Windermere, and with my headaches now cleared up, and most of the stiffness gone from my neck, I am looking forward to riding again — though I must say I wouldn't at all mind another seven days off some time soon!

MAY

THURSDAY 1 MAY

The show is back on the road ... and what a bloody show it is! Despite a vague attempt at evasion, I had to undertake the three-hour cross-country drive to Hereford for a single ride in their first race, then head south for two more at Wincanton's evening meeting. None of them obliged — and I fear life is going to continue in this vein for the remaining month of the season, because, all too often, I will be chalked down to ride moderate horses at two meetings in a day.

Events would have been far more tolerable, however, had I not bumped into Matt McCourt, the Oxfordshire trainer, in the car park at Wincanton. He told me that Graham, his son, had broken his wrist, and asked me to step in for the ride on Oyster Pond. I should have known better, but I reasoned that this was a reliable old handicapper he was asking me to ride, and he might even win; needless to say, he didn't. At the second-last ditch he stumbled on landing, and I ended up on the deck, bringing down two following horses as I fell. I got a very unpleasant kick on the side, and although the doctor did not sign me off, my hip-bone currently looks as if it has got a football attached. All in all, I think I prefer being on 'holiday' in the Lakes!

FRIDAY 2 MAY

I am too old for these double-shift days. Today it was Plumpton followed by Taunton — one ride at each and an endless drive in between. My hip had loosened up last night, aided by a whisky or two and a few dances at Stringfellows, the London nightspot, but I still had a huge and colourful bruise to show off in the weighing-room before going out to win on Gavin's Boom Patrol. I had been

156

concerned that a longish break, and a couple of outings on the flat, might have turned him against hurdling; but, oddly, he has never jumped better, and I could not have won by less than 20 lengths if I had tried. I fancied completing a long-range double with my one ride at Taunton, but got beaten into second. Exhaustion had by then set in, and rather than flog back to Newmarket through the night, I booked in at Torquay. Graham Bradley stayed down, too, and it was a thoroughly good decision.

SATURDAY 3 MAY

The rains have ended and the ground is drying fast all round the country. Last time I was at Taunton, little more than a week ago, they needed a tractor to tow vehicles out of the mud in the car-park, but last night it was rock-hard. The ground was firm at Worcester tonight, too, and I think the runners will quickly diminish from now on in.

At the end of a week which has taken me to virtually every corner of England — I hate to think what my mileage has been — there was another frustration in store when I got beaten a short-head on Welsh Oak tonight. Just to sum up the way luck runs in cycles, 'Scu', for whom nothing can go wrong right now, finished second in the novice chase, and then got the race on an objection to move even farther clear at the top of the championship.

Yet again, I failed to get home. This time, it was my old pal Johnny Burke who kept me out — and eventually put me up for the night. I always enjoy 'Burkey's' company, and it is good news that he is to start training next season. Many try and fail, but Johnny will not lack for knowledge or effort.

SUNDAY 4 MAY

My Bank Holiday plans were all made in advance. I was to go to the mixed meeting at Haydock to ride two horses for Nick Henderson and one for Mick Naughton. It is the last really valuable meeting of the season, also the last televised jumping, and I was looking forward to it. But soon after ten this morning Nick phoned to tell me he had taken his two horses out and he wanted me to go and ride one at Fontwell instead, which won't seem quite the same. I then had to spend an hour on the phone trying to scrape one or two more rides together to make the journey viable. I ended up with a tally of three, but I can't see any of them winning.

After that, it was to lunch on the lawn at James Toller's house. James is one of the young and friendly Newmarket flat trainers, but he had invited a whole bevy of 'hooray henries' who, I'm afraid, took a considerable amount of stick from me. The Pimms flowed very freely. It was also very well mixed, and by mid-afternoon I was all for taking on the world at snooker. I settled for a couple of bloodstock agents I know, thinking they would be easy meat for a few quid but, what with my lack of recent practice and the Pimms (and the scotch which followed) I soon discovered I could hardly see a ball, let alone pot one. I lost.

MONDAY 5 MAY

There is a moral here somewhere, if only I can find it. Mike Furlong and I were both called before the stewards at Fontwell for the 'crime' of failing to do up our chinstraps as we mounted our horses. We were each asked if we had anything to say. I said no, but he launched into an elaborate and prolonged account of why his mind had been elsewhere. The net result? I was fined £50, and so was he!

I had plenty of time to mull over the implications of this. I spent most of the evening drumming my fingers on the steering wheel as the Bank Holiday traffic crawled ponderously away from the Sussex coast. I was not even nourished by a winner; Nick's Master Bob, carrying 12 stone, was caught on the line and beaten a short-head, just when I thought my journey had been worthwhile after all.

TUESDAY 6 MAY

Ana Wasslaawi had not been seen out since pulling himself up at Chepstow just before Christmas. He has been gelded since and, although he still acts the monkey at home, Nick ran him at Kempton tonight in the hope that he might reform and deign to show the limitless ability he possesses. It was a vain hope. The horse at first refused to take any interest, then, after I had somehow forced him over two flights of hurdles, he switched on and raced impressively to the third last. I was lying second now, thinking I might win, but as soon as I made the initial twitch towards asking him the question, he dug his toes in again and I had to pull him up before the second last.

He will doubtless now be called one of racing's great rogues, but I am not so sure. I remember a horse called Oscar Wilde, once trained by Fred Winter. He too had plenty of talent but often looked markedly reluctant to show it. He was sold on to John Jenkins' yard and, one day, they found him dead in his box. When the vet opened him up he discovered the poor animal had only one kidney — and that was shrivelled to the size of a walnut. While the pundits had been labelling him a thief and the punters had been much less polite, Oscar Wilde must have been in terrible pain every time he ran a race. I just wonder whether something similarly serious is amiss with Ana Wasslaawi, because I have never believed horses are clever enough to behave as he is doing.

WEDNESDAY 7 MAY
No racing. I tried three times to cut the lawns, but each time I wheeled out the mower and prepared to start, down came the rain. I'm sure this is the complaint of many more serious gardeners than me in this oddly unco-operative spring. It didn't break my heart — I simply gave up and read a book instead.

THURSDAY 8 MAY
It may sound like wishing life away, but I think I am in the majority among the jockeys I know in longing for the end of the month, the end of the season. Ten months of racing six days a week, with all the driving it entails, is perhaps a more demanding season than any other sport requests of its principals. Almost every year, May becomes a drag for me, a month in which incentives are few and time is for killing.

FRIDAY 9 MAY
Indamelody has cropped up regularly in the pages of this diary, not because he is one of my favourite horses but because he is certainly one of the most challenging and interesting rides in Nicky Henderson's yard. A very capable handicapper over hurdles, he has not exactly taken eagerly to fences, yet he undeniably has ability. Last month at Nottingham I got him safely round — with him, the most important obstacle overcome — and then made up ground rapidly on the run-in to win a novice chase.

159

This, I felt, had done the horse's confidence immeasurable good, but when he next ran, burdened with a heavy weight, Nick decided to take a few pounds off his back by giving the ride to our claimer, Mike Bowlby. Now Mike is a very decent little rider, but I would maintain that Indamelody is not a boy's ride, and it is not pique at having lost the ride which prompts me to report I was not at all surprised when the combination ended up on the floor. I was, however, dismayed, wondering whether the tender work we had done on the horse's confidence would now be laid to waste. Today at Stratford I was to find out.

For the first time, Indamelody was declared for a handicap chase, running against horses far more experienced than him over fences. Despite that, the punters made him favourite on the strength of his two novice wins and, it must be said, his almost irrelevant hurdles form. I was not so confident. Stratford is a tight little circuit where horses can often rush at the fences so, in the circumstances, I was delighted when my horse finished a close-up third, having jumped well until he got a bit low over the last two. We may yet get another race out of him before the season is over.

SATURDAY 10 MAY

My choice of how to spend the day was straightforward enough: accept the six-hour round trip for two rides at Hereford, neither of which had any real chance; or stay at home with my feet up watching the cup final on TV. I did not find it very difficult to plump for the latter, but I confess to having a few pangs of guilt as the day progressed. Was I doing the right thing? Was it natural to feel lethargic at this end of the long season, or was I verging on the unprofessional? I put such thoughts out of my mind, enjoyed a splendid cup final, and saw with some relief that neither horse was placed.

SUNDAY 11 MAY

The morning papers gave me depressing food for thought. An amateur jockey named Michael Blackmore was killed by a fall at Market Rasen's evening meeting last night. I have never met him, indeed I don't think I had ever heard of him until now, but the news is still stunning. There is no escaping the conclusion that it could happen to any of us tomorrow. There but for the grace of God. . . .

Two better pieces of news on the social front — my old snooker partner Tommy Keddie is coming back to town after a brief and abortive move to Carlisle, so Sunday evenings will soon revert to their previous pleasurable pattern at the Willie Thorne Snooker Centre; and, much to my surprise, an invitation to Robert Sangster's 50th birthday party has flopped onto my door-mat. It is in two weeks' time on the Isle of Man and I have a sus-picion it could be quite a thrash.

MONDAY 12 MAY

I spent the entire day in my armchair reading a Jack Higgins novel called *Solo*. This time, there were no pangs of guilt what-soever.

TUESDAY 13 MAY

Bad news from home: one of my aunts has died, the second family death in a couple of months. As we are a close family, and as there is some sorting out to be done, with no racing to concern me today I drove up to Derbyshire to lend a hand.

THURSDAY 15 MAY

Jeff King and I have been friends for years. When he was riding I openly admired his ability. To me, he was among the top two or three jockeys around. I also appreciated his sense of humour and the uninhibited way in which he lived his life, never being afraid to say what he thought and always being around to buy a drink in the bar at the end of a long day. There are now too few around like 'Kingy' and I have to say I may even have modelled myself on him a little. But, with all that said, he can also be the most infuri-ating bloke I know, especially when he takes the berating of beaten jockeys to extremes. Tonight was just such an example.

I had wanted to do both meetings today, taking in a ride for Jeff at Ludlow before coming on to Uttoxeter for the evening card. In the end I had to settle for riding one of Nicky's novice chasers at the Uttoxeter course, which at least meant I could pick up my parents and give them an evening's racing to help take their mind off their recent troubles.

I was on my way back to the weighing-room after being well beaten on Nick's horse when someone hailed me. It was Jeff, asking if I was all right to ride a horse called Kings Jug for him in the handicap chase. I agreed, and if I lacked a little enthusiasm, I certainly listened when he told me he thought the horse had every chance of winning. The race, however, never went to plan at all, and although Kings Jug made up a stack of ground in the straight and finished fastest of all, I knew that Jeff was not going to be ecstatic.

I was right. He was, in fact, in a fury, and I was the one on the end of his temper. Maybe he was right, maybe I had not ridden the greatest of races; but I had never even sat on the horse before and I had discovered he had a mind of his own. He was not an easy ride, and I felt I did not deserve quite such a bollocking. When it continued in the weighing-room a few minutes later I began to get very angry myself and we might easily have come to blows.

Every trainer is entitled to tell a jockey exactly what he thinks of the ride he has given his horse. Many never accept that entitlement, keeping their thoughts to themselves, while most others get the criticism out of the way and then forget it. This time I believe Jeff went too far, and even if he had right on his side I don't feel I should be spoken to quite like that. I wonder if I will ride for him again?

FRIDAY 16 MAY
The compensations of night racing in May occasionally come in the shape of a good social evening to follow. Tonight, for instance, I rode two bad novice hurdlers for Nicky and then, in company with Dermot Browne, set off to examine what Stratford had to offer. We found two good pubs and then, with a journey to Bangor facing us tomorrow, put up for the night at the Moat House Hotel, set on the banks of the Avon.

SATURDAY 17 MAY
Dermot had taken a bad fall last night, suffering a few kicks after hitting the deck. He felt better after a drink or two but a night's sleep in a strange bed had stiffened him up again and, half-way to

Bangor, he was plainly in agony and in no state to even consider riding today. So he had to come just for the trip — which was virtually what I did, too. Torrential rain ruined the chances of my two rides, so I set off for the cross-country dash back to the evening meeting at Warwick in a dismal mood, made worse when I got there to find one of my two mounts had been taken out. I was left with Bluelimit, top weight in the handicap hurdle, and after two or three hard recent races he just couldn't cope with the ground and the extra poundage on his back. He did not, however, go down without incident.

Three from home I was still going well as a gap opened up on the inner. It was only a narrow gap, but it was a good position, and race-riding tactics dictated that I should try to get there. As I made my move, with the hurdle looming, I could sense someone else had the same idea, but I had to keep going. I got there first and the other fellow, with nowhere to go, crashed out through the wing of the hurdle. It turned out to be Kevin Mooney and, thankfully, there was not much damage. No blame was attached. He understood, as would any good jockey, that this was a classic 'him or me' situation in which someone has to lose out.

The jockeys' title race has taken an interesting turn. It had looked to be in Peter Scudamore's pocket, but after a lean week or two for him it is not so clear. 'Sharky' Sherwood has been banging in the winners relentlessly and after winning the first at Warwick tonight he was only six behind. I could well imagine 'Scu' jumping up and down in frustration as he had visions of another championship vanishing at the last but, having taken on the daunting drive to Newcastle to ride one for his good mate Nigel Twiston-Davies, the gods smiled on him. Not only did that one win, but he picked up a spare ride on that grand old chaser Silent Valley — and got that one home, too. So, at eight winners ahead and with only a fortnight left, I reckon P. Scudamore is the new champion.

TUESDAY 20 MAY
The things I do for a game of tennis! Newton Abbot's final two-day meeting began today, and none of my regular employers were running anything, but by scrubbing around on the phone I

managed to pick up a ride for Jimmy Frost, an old friend, basically to ensure I could get down to the Palace Hotel for the last
time this season. I was expecting no more than the £50 riding fee
as recompense for the journey so it was to my great surprise when
Stars and Stripes — who began the race with a series of duck-eggs
next to his name in the form guide — responded to an energetic
finish on my part and won the handicap hurdle.

WEDNESDAY 21 MAY
My two rides at today's evening meeting were previously
unknown to me and, frankly, I shall shed no tears if I never see
either of them again. They certainly made it an eventful night.

The first of them was for Cheltenham trainer Owen O'Neill.
The girl leading the horse around the parade ring warned me that
he was 'a bit keen' but this did not exactly set alarm bells ringing
in my head. It is the type of comment a jockey very often hears
from proud, committed stable staff. This one, however, happened
to have understated the case.

The routine at Newton Abbot is that, before cantering down
to the two-mile start, jockeys take their mounts past the stands to
show them the last hurdle. My horse was a shade impatient. We
were, remember, approaching the hurdle from the 'wrong' side —
in other words, it was leaning towards us, but this animal wanted
to jump the thing and nothing I could do would deter him. He had
taken off. So, hanging on and hoping, we ploughed through the
hurdle, the horse miraculously kept his feet and I belatedly
managed to get a stranglehold on him and get him down to the
start. He jumped well enough in the race, too, but could finish
only fourth. Maybe he prefers his hurdles back to front!

After that little episode I was all for a quiet ride round in the
last race of the night, when I was chalked up for another of
Jimmy Frost's horses. I had not expected, however, to earn my
riding fee quite so easily. This one, called Getaway though
heaven knows why, was a lazy sort and Jimmy told me to wear a
pair of spurs to wake him up. They made absolutely no difference. When the tapes went up, he plodded three strides and then
mulishly refused to go another yard. Variety, they say, is the spice
of life. After tonight, I am not so sure.

FRIDAY 23 MAY

The sun shone at last, so the golf clubs came out of hiding. Today's racing for me was an evening card at Towcester, so I had plenty of time for a round on the Newmarket course ... which was just as well, the way I play.

I have just one ride tonight — Indamelody. He was back over hurdles again but he has had his fair share of work this season and I feared he might just have gone over the top. The way he ran, dying under me from the third last, I was right.

SATURDAY 24 MAY

In any rating of the 1986 social calendar, I guess Robert Sangster's 50th birthday party will be upstaged only by the Royal Wedding. It lived up to expectations in every way and was, quite simply, the most memorable shindig I have ever been privileged to attend.

This was, of course, a racing day and I had to back out of a couple of rides at Warwick, one of them for my guv'nor Nick — but, as he was heading for the Isle of Man too, I think he felt he couldn't complain. So, at 6.00 p.m., a crowd of us boarded a specially chartered Boeing 737 at Gatwick and the party was underway. I must say I could easily have foregone the next bit, as landing a thing of that size on the tiny Manx airstrip would be hair-raising at the best of times, let alone in driving rain. But we survived, and after a rapid change of clothes at the Golf Links Hotel to which Di and I had been billetted, it was on to the palatial Sangster residence, where an enormous marquee had been erected in the grounds.

The guest list extended to something over 500 and, by the look of the place, there had been very few regrets. The cream of the racing world was present, and if I was surprised to find myself the only National Hunt jockey there, I did not let this detract from the enjoyment. Paul Anka's cabaret, Charlie Benson's uproarious speech and a constant flow of pink champagne all stand out as memories, and as night became morning the celebrations continued unabated. It was around 6.00 a.m., and the birds were singing, when we finally pulled up stumps and staggered back to bed. Quite a night!

165

SUNDAY 25 MAY

Part two of the Sangster celebrations was as impressive as part one. Food and yet more drinks (champagne naturally) were provided at our hotel from 12.30 p.m., so I was out of bed just in time to partake, and then the party moved on to Castletown race course for the Isle of Man's big Derby meeting. I had been asked to ride in the hurdles race, but decided I would enjoy the social side of the weekend instead. When I saw how tight the track was, I felt I had made the correct decision. Robert's horse won the Manx Derby so more champagne arrived. Really, considering I have only met him socially a few times, I feel quite honoured to be part of the enclave at this gathering.

It ended for the night at the Palace Casino and, as I have to ride tomorrow, I exerted some self-discipline and went to bed at midnight. Just before I retired, Nicky started to give me my riding instructions for tomorrow. It was a good job Di was beside me, because they would quickly have faded into a sleepy oblivion otherwise.

MONDAY 26 MAY

I proved today that, whatever others may think, my social life never affects my riding — and then I proved the maxim that you never can tell what is around the next corner.

I felt a degree or two short of death when I dragged myself and Di out of bed at 6.00 a.m. for the early flight back to Gatwick but, in the true spirit of 'the old Ecc', I kept kicking. Di dropped out of the day as soon as we got home, taking to her bed again, but I went on to Huntingdon and proceeded to ride two winners for Nick. If I say so myself, I rode them both like a demon and no one was more aware than me of their significance. Nick and Fred Winter, to whom he was once assistant trainer, have for the past month been fighting quite a scrap over the trainers' championship. Fred, never one to be beaten lightly, sent out nine horses today at five meetings, and Nick badly needed some winners to stay in front. Well, only one of Fred's troops came home victorious, so my double, and a win for Master Bob at Fontwell, makes virtually certain that I am now retained jockey at jumping's champion stable.

I was feeling pretty bucked by all this as I went out for my last ride of the day. John Jenkins' State Diplomacy went off as favourite for the handicap hurdle, so I thought I had every chance of riding my first treble of the season. I should have known better. We got no further than the second flight. Something fell in front of us, we were brought down, and another horse crashed on top of us ... or so I'm told. To be honest I remember very little about it, because for the first time in my career I was unconscious.

They tell me I was still motionless as the remaining runners passed me on the next circuit. They also tell me I came round in time to tell the ambulance staff what they could do with their stretcher. The upshot, naturally, was a seven-day rest period for my second bout of concussion inside a month. So that's it: end of story, end of season. The highs and the lows of this funny old game, all captured in a single afternoon.

TUESDAY 27 MAY
I had planned to finish the season this weekend with a trip to Sweden, where I have been offered good rides in their Grand National and Champion Hurdle. That must now go by the board. Quite apart from the concussion, an x-ray in Cambridge today confirmed that I have also cracked a rib. My main worry now is whether I will be fit enough to fly to Australia with the British team next week. I spent much of the afternoon in hot baths trying to soothe away the worst of the aches.

WEDNESDAY 28 MAY
I did nothing today because I was not up to doing anything. My head is still woozy, my brain working slowly as if scrambled. And I don't recommend cracked ribs, either. It is not just the energetic pursuits which have to be scrubbed from the agenda — I can't even sneeze or laugh.

THURSDAY 29 MAY
My ribs are feeling easier, my head is slowly clearing and I'm on my way to London for the annual social gathering of 300 jump jockeys at the Sportsman Club awards dinner. It is a great gesture by Max Kingsley and his directors to give these awards every

167

year, though I wonder if they realise what havoc they are turning loose on the West End when the ceremony is over?

I had another cheque to pick up for finishing third in the championship with 63 winners. I had a good year. Yes, of course I fancied being champion, but in all honesty there was hardly a stage of the season when I considered myself favourite. First Simon, who had a fantastic first season as a professional, built up a good lead and then 'Scu' came with a rattle. A place in the top three was always the best I could hope for, but I did have the satisfaction of winning some big races along the way. Also, despite my current state, I finished up in one piece. I had two rounds of concussion, a cracked rib, a damaged ankle and various bruises, but when I think of Sam Morshead, Mark Perrett and Anthony Webber, I think myself very lucky.

As my season ends I feel like the hero in *Papillon*, the Frenchman who keeps escaping from prison and, in the closing shots, gets away from Devil's Island, from where no one has ever escaped before. He has made a coconut raft and he is floating out to sea, lying on his belly. Suddenly, he looks up at the sky, shakes his fist and bellows defiantly: 'I'm still here, you bastard'.

STATISTICS

HOW THE JOCKEYS FINISHED 1985/86 SEASON

	1st	2nd	3rd	Unplaced	Total
P. Scudamore	91	61	52	335	539
S. Sherwood	79	50	53	181	363
S. Smith Eccles	63	47	32	184	326
H. Davies	58	45	30	264	397
R. Dunwoody	55	51	61	337	504
R. Rowe	48	48	42	240	378
R. Lamb	46	34	31	163	274
C. Grant	42	49	37	194	322
J.J. O'Neill	38	35	27	162	262
G. McCourt	38	43	28	217	326

BIG RACE WINNERS 1985/86 SEASON

MACKESON GOLD CUP HANDICAP CHASE $2^{1}/_{2}$m
(Cheltenham, Nov 9)
1. Half Free 9-11-10   R. Linley 9-2
2. Newlife Connection 6-10-2   S. Sherwood 5-1
3. Another City 6-10-1   P. Tuck 12-1
Distances: head, 8L. Winner trained by F. Winter. 10 ran

HENNESSY COGNAC GOLD CUP HANDICAP CHASE 3m 2f 82yds
(Newbury, Nov 23)
1. Galway Blaze 9-10-0   M. Dwyer 11-2
2. Run And Skip 7-10-9   S. Morshead 7-1
3. Door Latch 7-10-8   R. Rowe 9-1
Distances: 12L, 5L. Winner trained by J. FitzGerald. 15 ran.

169

STILL FORK TRUCKS GOLD CUP HANDICAP CHASE 2¹/₂m
(Cheltenham, Dec 7)
1. Combs Ditch 9-11-9   C. Brown 13-2
2. Final Argument 9-10-11   P. Tuck 9-4 fav
3. Western Sunset 9-11-5   R. Dunwoody 9-2
Distances: 7L, 5L. Winner trained by D. Elsworth. 7 ran.

CORAL WELSH GRAND NATIONAL HANDICAP CHASE 3³/₄m
(Chepstow, Dec 21)
1. Run And Skip 7-10-8   P. Scudamore 13-1
2. Golden Ty 7-9-11   Mr. A. Orkney 100-1
3. Kumbi 10-10-3   S. Smith Eccles 18-1
Distances: 6L, 2L. Winner trained by J. Spearing. 18 ran.

KING GEORGE VI CHASE 3m
(Kempton, Dec 26)
1. Wayward Lad 10-11-10   G. Bradley 12-1
2. Combs Ditch 9-11-10   C. Brown 3-1
3. Earls Brig 10-11-10   T.G. Dun 7-1
Distances: neck, 12L. Winner trained by Mrs. M. Dickinson. 5 ran.

ANTHONY MILDMAY, PETER CAZALET MEMORIAL
HANDICAP CHASE 3m 5f 18yds
(Sandown, Jan 4)
1. Run And Skip 8-11-1   P. Scudamore 7-2
2. Contradeal 9-10-0   S. Shilston 5-2 fav
3. Buckbe 7-10-0   C. Brown 10-1
Distances: ¹/₂L, 2L. Winner trained by J. Spearing. 8 ran.

EMBASSY PREMIER CHASE FINAL 2¹/₂m
(Ascot, Jan 11)
1. Very Promising 8-11-10   P. Scudamore 5-4 fav
2. Mr Moonraker 9-11-10   B. Powell 9-1
3. I Haventalight 7-11-10   S. Sherwood 10-1
Distances: short head, 10L. Winner trained by D. Nicholson. 8 ran.

OTELEY HURDLE 2m
(Sandown, Feb 1)
1. See You Then 6-11-12   S. Smith Eccles 3-1
2. Sabin Du Loir 7-10-7   G. Bradley 7-2
3. Tom Sharp 6-11-0   P. Tuck 4-1
Distances: 2¹/₂L, ¹/₂L. Winner trained by N. Henderson. 9 ran.

WILLIAM HILL IMPERIAL CUP HANDICAP HURDLE 2m
(Sandown, Mar 8)
1. Insular 6-9-10   E. Murphy 14-1
2. Hypnosis 7-10-2   C. Brown 11-1

3. Peter Martin 5-10-2   K. Mooney 14-1
Distances: $^3/_4$L, neck. Winner trained by I. Balding. 19 ran.

WATERFORD CRYSTAL SUPREME NOVICES HURDLE 2m
(Cheltenham, Mar 11)
1. River Ceiriog 5-11-8   S. Smith Eccles 40-1
2. Deep Idol 6-11-8   N. Madden 4-1 fav
3. The Clown 5-11-8   R. Stronge 100-1
Distances: 15L, $1^1/_2$L. Winner trained by N. Henderson. 29 ran.

ARKLE CHALLENGE TROPHY CHASE 2m
(Cheltenham, Mar 11)
1. Oregon Trail 6-11-8   R. Beggan 14-1
2. Charcoal Wally 7-11-8   B. Powell 11-1
3. Desert Orchid 7-11-8   C. Brown 11-2
Distances: $^3/_4$L, 8L. Winner trained by S. Christian. 14 ran.

WATERFORD CRYSTAL CHAMPION HURDLE 2m
(Cheltenham, Mar 11)
1. See You Then 6-12-0   S. Smith Eccles 5-6 fav
2. Gaye Brief 9-12-0   P. Scudamore 14-1
3. Nohalmdun 5-12-0   J.J. O'Neill 20-1
Distances: 7L, $1^1/_2$L. Winner trained by N. Henderson. 23 ran.

QUEEN MOTHER CHAMPION CHASE 2m
(Cheltenham, Mar 12)
1. Buck House 8-12-0   T. Carmody 5-2
2. Very Promising 8-12-0   P. Scudamore 11-2
3. Kathies Lad 9-12-0   S. Smith Eccles 11-1
Distances: 3L, 8L. Winner trained by M. Morris. 11 ran.

DAILY EXPRESS TRIUMPH HURLDE (4-y-o) 2m
(Cheltenham, Mar 13)
1. Solar Cloud 11-0   P. Scudamore 40-1
2. Brunico 11-0   D. Browne 16-1
3. Son Of Ivor 11-0   T. Carmody 16-1
Distances: $^3/_4$L, short head. Winner trained by D. Nicholson. 28 ran.

TOTE CHELTENHAM GOLD CUP CHASE $3^1/_4$m
(Cheltenham, Mar 13)
1. Dawn Run 8-11-9   J.J. O'Neill 15-8 fav
2. Wayward Lad 11-12-0   G. Bradley 8-1
3. Forgive 'N' Forget 9-12-0 M. Dwyer 7-2
Distances: 1L, $2^1/_2$L. Winner trained by P. Mullins. 11 ran.

JAMESON IRISH GRAND NATIONAL HANDICAP CHASE $3^1/_2$m
(Fairyhouse, Mar 31)
1. Insure 8-9-11   M. Flynn 16-1

2. Omerta 6-9-9   Mr. L. Wyer 4-1
3. Bold Agent 10-9-7   J.P. Byrne 16-1
Distances: 10L, 8L. Winner trained by P. Hughes. 15 ran.

CAPTAIN MORGAN AINTREE LIMITED HANDICAP CHASE 2m
(Liverpool, Apr 5)
1. Kathies Lad 9-10-13   S. Smith Eccles 11-8 fav
2. Lefrak City 9-10-7   H. Davies 7-2
3. Badsworth Boy 11-11-10   R. Earnshaw 4-1
Distances: $2^{1}/_{2}$L, $^{1}/_{2}$L. Winner trained by A.P. Jarvis. 6 ran.

SANDEMAN AINTREE HURDLE 2m 5f 110yds
(Liverpool, Apr 5)
1. Aonoch 7-11-9   J. Duggan 16-1
2. See You Then 6-11-11   S. Smith Eccles 4-9 fav
3. Sheer Gold 6-11-1   G. Bradley 6-1
Distances: 1L, 15L. Winner trained by Mrs. S. Oliver. 9 ran.

SEAGRAM GRAND NATIONAL HANDICAP CHASE $4^{1}/_{2}$m.
(Liverpool, Apr 5)
1. West Tip 9-10-11   R. Dunwoody 15-2
2. Young Driver 9-10-0   C. Grant 66-1
3. Classified 10-10-3   S. Smith Eccles 22-1
Distances: 2L, 20L. Winner trained by M. Oliver. 40 ran.

WHITBREAD GOLD CUP HANDICAP CHASE 3m 5f 18yds
(Sandown, Apr 26)
1. Plundering 9-10-6   S. Sherwood 14-1
2. Buckbe 7-10-7   B. Powell 15-2
3. Arctic Beau 8-10-0   R. Dunwoody 9-1
Distances: $^{1}/_{2}$L, 15L. Winner trained by F. Winter. 16 ran.

SWINTON INSURANCE BROKERS TROPHY HANDICAP
HURDLE 2m
(Haydock, May 5)
1. Prideaux Boy 8-11-2   M. Bowlby 15-2
2. Gala's Image 6-10-7   H. Davies 9-1
3. Janus 8-10-3   M. Hammond 25-1
Distance: $2^{1}/_{2}$L, 6L. Winner trained by C. Roach. 20 ran.

INDEX

173

174